Introduction to Ebonics

The Relexification of African Grammar with English and Other Indo-European Words

(Volume I)

Linda Redmond Taylor

Ernie A. Smith, Special Linguistic Consultant and Contributing Author

FOREWORD: Molefi K. Asante, Ph.D.
INTRODUCTION: Ernie A. Smith, Ph.D
SPECIAL CONTRIBUTING AUTHOR: Robert L. Williams, Ph.D.

Published and Distributed by:
Professional Publishing House, LLC
1425 W. Manchester Ave. Ste B
Los Angeles, California 90047
323-750-3592
Email: professionalpublishinghouse@yahoo.com
www.professionalpublishinghouse.com

Copyright © 2016 by Linda Redmond Taylor
Memphis, Tennessee
All rights reserved
Printed and Bound in the United States of America

Cover design: TWA Solutions
First printing October 2016
978-0-692-79600-9
10987654321

For inquiries contact: duhtruff@aol.com

CONTENTS

Contributing Authors--- v

Dedications (See Appendix I)

Tributes (See Appendix II)

Reasons for Writing *Introduction to Ebonics* ----------------- viii

Acknowledgements --xiv

Preface -- 1
Molefi Kete Asante

Introduction --- 3
Ernie A. Smith

Origin of the Word Ebonics --------------------------------- 6

1: Ebonics: The Pidgin-Creole Theory ----------------------- 16
Ernie A. Smith

2: Ebonics: Re-Claiming and Re-Defining Our Language----61
Robert L. Williams

3: Ebonics Is Most Relevant -------------------------------- 80

4: Etymologically African ---------------------------------- 99

5: Relexification---108

Twelve Commandments for Teaching an Ebonics-Speaking Child---133

APPENDICES

Appendix I: An Anthology of Dedications --------------------139

Appendix II: Tributes ------------------------------------144

Appendix III: The Naming of this Book ----------------------151

Appendix IV: Resolution No. 9697-0063-Oakland
Unified School District ----------------------------------153

Appendix V: Revised Ebonics Resolution No. 9697-0063------156

Appendix VI: Linguistic Society of America Resolution on the
Oakland Ebonics Issue ------------------------------------159

Appendix VII: Overview of Volume II ----------------------161

About the Author ---------------------------------------163

Relevant Bibliography -----------------------------------164

CONTRIBUTING AUTHORS

Justice is elusive in the following characterizations of the Contributors: Their achievements and accomplishments are vastly beyond what these few pages are capable of expressing.

MOLEFI KETE ASANTE is Professor of African American Studies at Temple University, and the founder of the first Ph.D. Program in African American Studies in the United States of America. His other responsibilities include being a: Visiting Professor at Zhejiang University, Hangzhou, China; Professor Extraordinarius at the University of South Africa, Institute for African Renaissance; Member, Coordinator of Diaspora Intellectuals, Pan African Scientific Council, African Union; President of Molefi Kete Asante Institute, Philadelphia, Pennsylvania; and International Organizer, Afrocentricity International. Dr. Asante has authored over sixty books, and he has been invited to lecture and present speeches all over the world. He has been recognized for his teaching and scholarship abilities. He has supervised scores of dissertations, and has served his profession in various positions: He has been the editor of the JOURNAL OF BLACK STUDIES from 1969 to the present.

ERNIE A. SMITH is currently a research Professor of Medicine and Clinical Linguistics in the Department of Internal Medicine, Division of Geriatrics at Charles R. Drew University of Medicine and Science in Los Angeles, California. As an interdisciplinary scholar, with a specialty in Comparative Culture and a sub-specialty in Comparative Linguistics, Dr. Smith has conducted research and published works in several behavioral and social science disciplines while teaching a variety of behavioral science, humanities and social science courses. Until 1982, Dr. Smith was a full Professor of Linguistics, in the Department of Linguistics, at California State University at Fullerton. Since then, as a career shift into health and human services, Dr. Smith has pursued post-graduate studies and conducted research in the cognitive and linguistic development of the Black child, bio-psycho-social health and gerontology. Currently, Dr. Smith continues his research in comparative and cognitive linguistics with an emphasis on cultural and linguistic competency in medical and behavioral health care environments. As one of the original definers of the term, "Ebonics," Dr. Smith has been at the forefront of scholarly research on Ebonics for the last thirty-four years.

ROBERT L. WILLIAMS is currently Professor Emeritus of Psychology and African American Studies at Washington University in St. Louis, Missouri. He was the founding Director of Black Studies (1970-1974) and Full Professor of Psychology and African American Studies (1970-1992) at Washington University, St. Louis. Dr. Williams developed the Black Intelligence Test of Cultural Homogeneity and several other culturally specific tests concerning IQ testing of Blacks. He appeared as a guest on numerous talk shows, i.e., The Montel Williams Show, to discuss his findings. In addition, he has published over sixty professional articles and five books, including *Ebonics: The True Language of Black Folks* (1975). After creating/coining the term, Ebonics, in 1973, he appeared on the NBC News and Black Entertainment Television (BET) to discuss the term's meaning and implications for the teaching of the Black child. Dr. Williams specializes in the areas of Black Psychology, racism, cultural bias in testing, cultural diversity, Black language and Black child development. On October 15, 2011, Dr. Williams was inducted into the Arkansas Black Hall of Fame. He is currently writing his memoirs to be included in the Archives of the History of Psychology.

DEDICATIONS – See Appendix I

TRIBUTES – See Appendix II

ALPHA TRIBUTE: Rev. Dr. Jessie Redmond

OMEGA TRIBUTE: Mariah Wilson Redmond

SPECIAL TRIBUTE I: Dr. Robert L. Williams, Jr.

SPECIAL TRIBUTE II: Dr. Ernie A. Smith

SPECIAL TRIBUTE III: Dr. Molefi Kete Asante

SPECIAL TRIBUTE IV: Dr. Adrian Dove

Reasons for Writing *Introduction to Ebonics*

Introduction to Ebonics, Volume I will help parents, educators and clinicians decide where the Ebonics die will be cast: Is Ebonics a language unto itself, or is it a dialect of English? The five chapters that encompass *Volume I* of this total Work will not leave any stones unturned about what Ebonics is and what it is not. The **first** purpose for writing *Introduction to Ebonics, Volume I*, is to set the record straight about what Ebonics is: Is Ebonics **genetically** akin to the Indo-European languages, or is it **genetically** akin to the Niger-Congo African languages? That question will be resolved even by the undecided before the final page is turned. One thing is for sure: The two are not synonymous; Ebonics and, so-called, Black English or African American English are not synonyms of each other. Ebonics is an antagonistic term. It is a replacement term, and was never meant to be housed in the same thought processes as being akin to the Germanic language family to which English belongs (Smith, in Crawford, 2001, p. 126 – 127).

On the other hand, as great and mighty as Standard American English (SAE) is esteemed to be, the fact is, there are linguists who question the very existence of SAE. For example, positing SAE as a dialect that has no native speakers, Fromkin et al., in *An Introduction to Language*, (2003), view SAE as "a dialect of English that many Americans almost speak", and they further state that "SAE is an idealization" (Fromkin et al., 2003, p. 455). Fromkin et al. contend that 'nobody speaks the SAE dialect, and if somebody did, we would not know it because SAE is not defined precisely' (Fromkin et al., 2003, p. 455). "Even after a conference of teachers and linguists in the 1990's was held to come up with a precise definition of SAE, none was forthcoming" (Fromkin et al., 2003, p. 455). If SAE is English, then what is English? No one would seriously question that, throughout the world, English is widely used as the language of commerce and diplomacy. In the science of historical and comparative linguistics, it has been, irrefutably, established that the grammar of English is derived from German, but the bulk of the vocabulary is derived from Latin and French (See J.A. Christensen et al., 1978).

After reading *Introduction to Ebonics, Volume I* and, later, *Volume II*, everyone will have a made up mind about "the true language of Black folks". Fence-sitting will end. He or she will, either, choose to remain unmoved about the erroneous classification of the speech and language of Blacks in America, or he or she will bear witness that Ebonics is the linguistic continuation of Africa in Black America. After reading the thousands of authentic examples of Black speech and language in America in the total Work, from single words that feature the differences in the way Blacks and Caucasians sound when saying the same words, to the creation of morpho-syntactical word combinations devoid of English structures, will truly open-minded and open-spirited, intelligent people conclude that the structures and word strings resemble English *only* in lexicon? Will reason dictate that they determine that, sure enough, Ebonics is not English and that, as a neo-African language, Ebonics is not **genetically** akin to the Germanic language family (Nehusi, in Crawford, 2001, p. 56, 66-67)? Will others, still, view those same thousands of authentic examples of Black speech and language in America as English? As it was/is with the hideous acceptance of slavery, however, blindness is blindness. (Douglass, reprinted, 1962, p. 85.)

The **second** purpose for writing *Introduction to Ebonics* is to support Ebonics-speaking parents (who are not ashamed of their African ancestry, or the African-based grammar of their speech) in their quest to have their children's school systems offer English-as-a-Second Language (ESL) teaching strategies to their Ebonics-speaking children. After reading this Book, Black parents who speak Ebonics as their mother tongue/ home language will have the knowledge necessary to, without daunting fear, declare Ebonics (or whatever term they prefer that posits their home language as an African language system) as their home language on their school districts' home language identification or survey forms (HLS) – not English. This includes making a correction to the incorrect information that may have been submitted to the schools. There are ways to overcome a strong school challenge to your declaration; the primary way is to ask the school to administer an English proficiency test to your child. If the child passes, that will be something to shout about, making your child, at best, bilingual in his understanding of English and Ebonics. If the child fails, the school will be required to serve him/her in all areas of concern.

Currently, all school districts in the United States are mandated, by law, to have parents identify 1) 'the first language their child learned to speak; 2) the language the child speaks most often outside of school; and 3) the language the child uses to speak to adults in their home'. Black, Ebonics-speaking parents who decide to, willingly, declare Ebonics as their native language have the right to declare Ebonics as the native, home, and primary language of their children, also. More times than not, when a parent neglects to make that declaration, that the parent and the children's first language and home language is Ebonics, the disturbing result is that the child matriculates through his formative years mis-educated or undereducated. In later life, he may not be able to fully compete in the job market because his ability to use English may be limited. (See Chapter 3, "Ebonics Is Most Relevant", for more insight on this topic.)

The **third** purpose for which *Introduction to Ebonics* is written is to end the further destruction of tender Black children's self-esteems as they enter school systems that continue to view them as speaking a "bad", "broken" or "corrupt" form of the English language. Also, as a speech/language pathologist, I wanted to abate the monumental, widespread, false labeling of Black children (who speak Ebonics as their primary language, and who cannot read or write sufficiently using

English), as speech and/or language impaired, and/or specific learning disabled. If the truth was to be told, it would reveal that many of the children who are labeled as Special Education students really have not had the appropriate educational experiences. In other words, (and this may cause a bit of fallout) forget how, during all initial placement and/or reevaluation meeting, it is verified that "lack of instruction" is *not* one of the reasons for a child's disability. In many instances, that is not the truth!! Daey jehs ain't been taught right [They just have not been appropriately taught]!!

The **fourth** purpose for writing *Introduction to Ebonics* is to encourage all schools to activate their "child find" policies to identify the Ebonics-speaking students who are limited English proficient (LEP): They are the cut-ups and the students who are always in the principals' offices for disruptive behavior. They are the students who are continuously suspended for "insubordination". (See Tom Rudd's article, "Racial Disproportionality in School Discipline", 2014, to gain further insight into this national problem.) They are the fighters! Listen!! See!! Why do we turn deaf ears and blind eyes to their plights? They are the ones in the seventh grade who cannot read or write using English. Giving them a page of sentences to read written in English would be like giving me a page of German sentences to read. I might pick out the "the's", the "and's", or the "I's", but I would not be able to fluently read the German words on the page. I do not know the German language. (Now the school systems are doubling their efforts to, seemingly, deter the success of Black students by requiring that standardized tests be administered by computer, without assuring that the students have had classes to teach them the efficient use of a computer keyboard. One teacher un-reasoned, thusly: "They play those video games; they can, therefore, navigate the keyboard to pass these tests.")

The **fifth** reason *Introduction to Ebonics* is written is to allow those who work with children to establish competencies, and then improve their competencies in the area of service delivery to Black students, by using this Book as a means of upgrading their level of cultural sensitivity and awareness of the linguistic rules and communication styles of Ebonics: The **sixth** and final reason why *Introduction to Ebonics* is written is to further promote the Africological hope of the ultimate abolition of that brutal, cruel, mental form of slavery called illiteracy, and the final banishment of the Black child's inability to verbally communicate effectively. Then, that child will not be "left behind". May the spirit of Frederick Douglass be revived: For he realized that the 'secret of all slavery and of all oppression had its foundation in the pride, the power, and the avarice of man, not the ordination of the Almighty' (Douglass, reprinted in 1962, p. 85).

It is my hope that this Work will fully convince every reader that Ebonics is the "true language of Black folks" in America, and that the descendants of enslaved Africans in America will begin an educational renaissance or movement. It is my hope that the descendants of enslaved Africans in America will soar as eagles toward being more productive in the classroom and in the workforce. It is my desire that the descendants of enslaved Africans in America will become more secure in their psychological and sociological development. It is my desire that being taught the English language using ESL strategies will prove to be the missing component in the education and cognitive development of the Black child and Blacks, as a people, in the United States of America.

It is my desire that the descendants of enslaved Africans in America will learn to appreciate their speech differences as African linguistic retentions that are not speech defects in need of corrective therapy. On the other hand, it is my desire that Black students will be able to produce the English counterparts of the retained African sounds, after becoming fluent in the English language, as a second language, via ESL strategies, for greater success in school and in the job market. It is my desire that the descendants of enslaved Africans will view the mastery of the English language as an asset and empowerment, as they will, then, be able to choose when to use the established rules of English grammar, whereas, before, they had been at a handicap because they had not learned English; therefore, they could not choose to use it. This, in turn, will nudge Black people toward a deeper pride of their total African heritage, summed up in their African linguistic, culinary, artistic, oratorical, and musical (including vocal, rhythm and dance) skills.

In a nutshell, those are the reasons why this Work was published, to reach down and pull Black students, specifically, and all Black people, in general, up to where they belong: Into the arena of being productive citizens in America.

NOTE: *Within the community of Ebonics speakers, there are preferences for what the members are called, i.e., Negroes, Blacks, Africans in the Diaspora, Nigritians, descendants of enslaved Africans in America, United States slave descendants of African origin, African Americans, etc. Throughout this Work, each of these terms may be utilized, at various points, to refer to the same members. However, my desire is that none is offended. So, "charge it to my head and not my heart", as this Work goes forth and teaches all about Ebonics as a language spoken by Negroes, Blacks, Africans in the Diaspora, Nigritians, descendants of enslaved Africans in diaspora, and African Americans, specifically, in the United States of America.*

ACKNOWLEDGEMENTS

First, I am thankful for the Inspiration to write this vision down. Secondly, my husband, Bro. Franco, is my earthly, praying, bilingual (Ebonics and SAE speaking), strong tower of my life. I thank him for utterly supporting me, even when it seemed that this march against the ignorance of what Ebonics is was one of lunaticity, if I may use my personal language or idiolect. As Bro. Franco, who is a walking Ebonics dictionary, proofed the finished Product, he often commented, "Peas and rice, aine that nice." That was his stamp of approval for having been my labor coach (with Dr. Smith being the "physician") as we brought forth this Work.

Thirdly, our children who lived at home during the conception and gestation state of this Work, Darryl (LaTarsha), Paul (Ferron), Christian, "king" Josiah, and Jesse, have shown that there is hope for all Ebonics-speaking children in their quests to learn SAE -- they are great models of what bilingualism in Black American children means. (Thanks to Darryl, too, for entering the Ebonics data pertaining to the International Phonetic Alphabet *twice* on the computer for me.) Also, lastly, our children who did not get to taste of this Work in progress are Alicia, Christopher, Walter (Shelia), and Anthony, all of whom are great communicators.

Fourthly, I thank my sisters and their "preacher-pastor" husbands: Pastor Jimmie and Celia Burse of Jackson, MS, and Pastor Douglass and Jessie Mae Thompson of San Antonio, TX, for their support. I thank the whole Redmond clan, namely, my brothers, Edward, Jerry, and Robert (Sheena) Redmond, and the following people: all of my former co-workers at the Disabilities Component of the Shelby County Head Start Program (Memphis, TN), especially, Tammy Washington and Marian Dabney (deceased 2014); and all of the following Memphis, Tennessee residents: Dr. N. Charles Thomas, Dr. Cheryl Golden, Sis. Imani Ward, Mrs. Daisy Smith, Sandra and Raymond Henry, William and Margaret Hayes, Alfred Robinson, and Dr. Merlin Taylor, for love, concern, some proofreading, and/or prayers during the many changes that have occurred in this twenty-four year time frame. To the librarian at Mitchell High School in Memphis, Tennessee, Mr. Christopher Graham, thanks for being my sounding board on our lunch breaks. Also, Mr. Chris Murphy (art instructor) at Mitchell High School, Memphis, Tennessee, made a believer out of me that children learn the language that is spoken and heard in the environment in which it is spoken and heard. That's all I will say about that in regard to Mr. Murphy. I thank Michael Adrian Davis, of Memphis, Tennessee, wihf [with] his "M.A.D." self. He is still the baddes radio and television personality who is before, during, and after his time. He inspired this Work, also. God bless Dr. George and Deborah Grant of Granthouse Publishers in Jonesboro, AR, for their initial, tireless attempts to birth this Work. Dr. Rosie Milligan and her Professional Publishing House team, are due accolades, too, along with Jessica Tilles of TWA Solutions.

Lastly, I would be negligent if I did not also acknowledge these four people who earned their doctorates in the field of speech/language pathology or audiology, and who assisted me while I was a struggling graduate student at the University of Memphis: Dr. Robert Mayo; Dr. Margie Crawford; Dr. George Charpied; and Dr. Patricia Cole-Holliday. They were once, at various times, my 'very present helps in times of need'.

If I had it to do over again, I would. 'The earth was not made in a day', and neither was a comprehensive Work on Ebonics possible, even after twenty-four years of diligent research and organization. "No dictionary of a living tongue can ever be perfect, since while it is hastening to publication, some words are budding, and some are fading away" (Bryson, 1990). This first, representative edition of *Introduction to Ebonics*, in the form of *Volume*

I, therefore, is a long way from being "exhaustive". I am just grateful to have been used to further spread this "naked" truth to you. Stay tuned for *Volume II* in 2017 that will feature Chapters Six through Seventeen.

<u>Disclaimer Statement</u>: The opinions expressed herein are solely those of the contributors and the author. Each one holds responsibility for his/her own designated chapters, and for the information shared in those chapters only.

PREFACE

Molefi Kete Asante

The subject of Ebonics has become an issue in the American public, although it has long been a language spoken by the majority of African Americans. Linda Redmond Taylor's *Introduction to Ebonics: The Relexification of African Grammar with English and Other Indo-European Words, Volumes I* and *II*, seeks to clarify the issues surrounding the language, and to present a strong case for the understanding of this very powerful form of communication. She has written a formidable work which will last for a long time as a standard lexicon.

What is most intellectually stimulating is the extensive lexicon presented by Linda Redmond Taylor, perhaps the most comprehensive work of its type to date (forthcoming in *Volume II*). She has gleaned the language from its classical roots in the late 19th century and early 20th century, as well as the contemporary bases, to make a case for an extended lexicon of the language. Since the development of the intellectual discussions around this subject, it has become fashionable to delve into the origins and the provenance of the language. However, in the case of Linda Redmond Taylor's work, the idea has been to accept the fact that the language is real, fundamental, and the creative work of an industrious people. This realization, different from a mere interest in cute sayings, has made her work significant for the lay person as well as for the expert.

Furthermore, her collaboration with Dr. Ernie Smith, generally considered to be the greatest proponent of Ebonics in the United States, has heightened her capabilities in using all of the evidences and insights of the total population. This is her crowning achievement—the ability to bring together the questions of stylistics, amplifications, idiomatic expressions, and language of the sporting life (in *Volume II*) in ways that show the rich value of the lexicon. No language's lexicon is any

1

better linguistically than any others', and the lexicon of Ebonics is finely textured, euphonic, and rhythmic.

I am convinced that those who read this work will be surprised at the great depth of the language spoken by the majority of African Americans. While English remains the official language of the United States, the national language of African Americans is Ebonics.

This is a book of great depth with many philosophical assumptions and numerous insights into the nature of our lives. I believe that the examples given by the author are profound evidences that Ebonics is not English. When someone says in Ebonics "Back when . . ." it is categorically different from the English "A long time ago . . ." What Linda Redmond Taylor demonstrates by her skillful use of Ebonics and English is that the beauty which inheres in Ebonics is not just there because of the structure of the language, although one cannot deny that, but the beauty is also dependent upon the phonology. She provides the reader with ample opportunities to think of what is possible in the larger context of culture. After all, language is a function of culture, and if you do not understand the culture of the African American, you are apt never to understand the way we communicate, think, and behave.

There is no doubt in my mind that many teachers can learn from this book, and it should be a required primer for all of those who are working in neighborhoods with large numbers of African Americans. I am happy that such a book has finally been written, and I encourage you to read it with the sensitivity and enthusiasm that went into its creation.

INTRODUCTION

Ernie A. Smith

The study of African American speech has been, like the study of other aspects of African American culture and behavior, influenced by the ideologies of different periods and the ideological perspectives of the different language and culture scholars of these periods (Alleyne, 1971, p. 121). The concept of Ebonics, however, is predicated on the Africological thesis that, owing to their history as descendants of enslaved West and Niger-Congo Africans, to the extent that African Americans have been born into, reared in and compelled to live in de jure and de facto segregation or apartheid in linguistic environments that are different from the Euro-American English speaking population, African Americans do not acquire English as their primary language or mother tongue. The Africologists maintain that, predicated on an analysis of the sound system, word formation and rules of grammar, African Americans have retained a West and Niger-Congo African phonology and morpho-syntax in the substratum of their speech. Thus, based on their comparative linguistic studies and findings, Africologists contend that African American speech is the linguistic continuation of Africa in Black America.

It was the Africological scholars who developed the term Ebonics. Etymologically, a portmanteau compound of two words, "ebony", which means black, and "phonics", which means sounds, the term, Ebonics, means, literally, Black Sounds. The term Ebonics was actually coined in 1973 by Dr. Robert L. Williams, a professor of psychology at Washington University in St. Louis, Missouri, during a conference on the cognitive and linguistic development of the African American child. It must be understood that Ebonics is not a synonym for the appellations Black English, African American English, African American Vernacular

English or any other appellation that infers, inherently, that the native language of descendants of enslaved Niger-Congo Africans is a dialect of English and, hence, genetically related to the Germanic language family to which English belongs. In fact, the term Ebonics was coined in repudiation of any and all appellations or expressions which infer that a genetic kinship or familial affinity exists between the language of the descendants of enslaved Niger-Congo Africans and the Indo-European language continuum (See Williams and Rivers, 1975, p.100).

Squarely in the Afro-centric camp, Linda Redmond Taylor's present work, *Introduction to Ebonics: The Relexification of African Grammar with English and other Indo-European Words*, is, clearly, in the vein of the Africological theory. Taylor's work is to Ebonics what Lorenzo Turner's work, *Africanisms in the Gullah Dialect* (1949), was to the Gullah language.

Linda Taylor's work is in the tradition of the works of Melville Herskovitz in his work, *The Myth of the Negro Past (1941)*; Frantz Fanon in his work, *Black Skin, White Masks* (1952); Janheinz Jahn in his work, *Muntu: The New African Culture* (1958); Nathan Hare in his work, *Black Anglo Saxons* (1965); Adrian Dove's landmark work "The Dove Counter Balance Test of Mental Intelligence" (1968), which was dubbed by the New York Times and other popular magazines as "The Soul Folk's Chittlin Test" (1968); Mervyn Alleyne's *Linguistic Continuity of Africa in the Caribbean* (1971); Robert Twigg's *Pan-African Language in the Western Hemisphere* (1973); Ernie Smith's *Evolution and Continuing Presence of the African Oral Tradition in Black America* (1974); Robert Williams' *Ebonics: The True Language of Black Folk* (1975) and his "Black Intelligence Test of Cultural Homogeneity" (B.I.T.C.H.) (1975); Anita DeFrantz's "Coming to Cultural and Linguistic Awakening: An African and African American Educational Vision", included in *Reclaiming Our Voices: Bilingual Education, Critical Pedagogy and Praxis* (ed. by Dean Frederickson 1995); and Aisha Blackshire-Blay's work, "The Location of Ebonics Within the Framework of the Africological Paridigm" in *Journal of Black Studies,* (September, 1996). Taylor's work builds a formidable case against the Euro-centric myths concerning African American language. Unlike the work of Geneva Smitherman (*Black Talk,* 1994), and many other works published as dictionaries, glossaries and lexicons of Black American language, Taylor's *Introduction To Ebonics* is rooted in the linguistic thesis that all human languages have grammatical structures, and that the grammar of human languages is "the mental system that allows human beings to form and interpret words and sentences in their language" (O'Grady et al, 1993, pp. 3-4). As a mental system, the grammar of all human languages is viewed as having a deep structure and a surface structure. In the science of linguistics the grammatical system is divided into five components: 'phonetics', 'phonology', 'morphology', 'syntax' and 'semantics'. Taylor's *Introduction to Ebonics* posits the lexicons of human languages are more related to the surface structure than the deep structure. Therefore, while it is not denied that, in the United States, the bulk of the lexicon of Ebonics has been adopted from Indo-European languages, Taylor's *Introduction To Ebonics* presents the deep phonetic and deep phonological (grammatical) variations that distinguish the speech of descendents of enslaved Africans as an African language system that is not, genetically, related to the Germanic English language.

In sum, Taylor's list of words, phrases, sayings, idiomatic expressions, and grammatical variations interconnects the unique thinking and experience base of African Americans with their Niger-Congo African ancestors'. Linda Taylor's *Introduction to Ebonics* attests to the Africologist's postulation that "anything an African does is an African's doing," especially an African's futile attempt to mimic the, so-called, ideally competent English usage. As such, Linda Taylor's *Introduction to Ebonics* supports the Africologist's position that "the linguistic creativeness and linguistic creations of Africans in diaspora are African in origin". Taylor's *Introduction to Ebonics* lays the groundwork for a redefinition of African American language that legitimizes it as an African based language, rather than allowing the deficit model to persist.

The Origin of the Word Ebonics

"The controversy aroused when the very problem is broached attests its vitality and its importance" (Herskovits, 1958, p. 11).

The scientific definition of Ebonics will be proclaimed throughout this Work. Etymologically, Ebonics is a portmanteau, or "a compound of two words", 'Ebony' which means 'Black' and 'phonics' which means 'sounds' – hence 'Black-Sounds' (Williams, 1975, p. vi). When the term Ebonics was coined in 1973, the intent of the Black professionals who coined and defined the term Ebonics was to repudiate the term Black English. This outright repudiation also applies to any other appellation that infers inherently that the language of the descendants of enslaved Africans in America is a dialect or variety of English. Corroboration that the term Ebonics was coined in repudiation of the term Black English is provided by the creator of the term, Ebonics, Dr. Robert Williams, in the first book ever written on Ebonics entitled *Ebonics: The True Language of Black Folks* (1975). Dr. Williams states:

> At a recent conference entitled "Cognitive and Language Development of the Black Child" held in St. Louis, Missouri January 1973, a group of Black scholars pointed out that the cultural difference model contained more political and economic overtones than grammatical or phonological and syntactical considerations... For example it is still not resolved as to what Black English or non-standard English really is. Simpkins, R. Williams, and Gunnings (1971), Taylor (1973), Ron Williams (1973), Beryl Bailey (1973), Gilliam (1973), Holt

(1973), Smith (1973), Simpkins (t1973), Smitherman (1973), Sims (1973) Covington (1973), in a barrage of criticism held that the concept of Black English or non-standard English contains deficit model characteristics, and therefore must be abolished. Following considerable discussion regarding the language of Black people, the group reached a consensus to adopt the term Ebonics (combining Ebony and phonics or Black sounds). (p. 100)

Ebonics was clearly not English. As defined by Dr. Williams and crafted by linguist Ernie A. Smith, the following wording was declared to be the official definition of the term Ebonics.

Ebonics is defined as the linguistic and paralinguistic features which on a concentric continuum represent the communicative competence of West African, Caribbean, and United States slave descendants of African origin. Ebonics includes the various idioms, patois, argots, idiolects and social dialects of these people. It is thus the culturally appropriate language of Black people and is not considered to be deviant. (*Ebonics: The True Language of Black Folks*, 1975, p. 100)

Based on the irrefutable, scientific evidence presented as research findings by the comparative linguists and cognitive scientists that established the genetic linguistic link between the language of Blacks in America and the languages of West and Niger-Congo Africa, the term Ebonics was created to identify the language of the descendants of enslaved Africans as a language other than English. This is discussed by Subira Kifano and Ernie Smith in an article entitled "Ebonics and Education in the Context of Culture: Meeting the Language and

Cultural Needs of English Learning African American Students". As contributors to *Ebonics in the Urban Education Debate*, (Ramirez et al., 2000), Kifano and Smith state:

> [T]o reconstruct or trace the ancestral forms in any language or hybrid dialect to a given parent language family it must first and foremost be established that there is a 'common origin' or 'genesis' rooted in an identified 'common ancestor language'... [T]here must be evidence of a historical connectedness based on 'linguistic characteristics that are inherited by one generation of speakers from another, as opposed to those which are acquired from other sources'. (pp. 66-67)

Again, the term Ebonics was created in "repudiation" of the appellations Black English (BE), Non-Standard English (NSE), Non-Standard Negro English (NSNE), Black Vernacular English (BVE), African American English (AAE) or African American Vernacular English (AAVE). "[T]hose who use the term Ebonics as a synonym for BE, NSE, BVE, and AAVE, etc., are utterly misinformed and lack the will or skills to research its origin and true meaning" (Kifano and Smith, in Ramirez et al., 2000, p. 69). "... They all attempt to deny the very possibility of an Afrikan language and, therefore, the humanity of Afrikans and define the word from a Eurocentric and often a white supremacist viewpoint ..." (Nehusi, in Crawford, 2001, p. 75-76)

What home language, native language, or mother tongue do Black children, the descendants of enslaved Niger-Congo Africans in diaspora, speak? Do the majority of them speak English or one of its dialects? Do they speak Ebonics or Black Sounds? Various studies indicate that parents, educators and clinicians need closure to the wide scope of information that has been uncovered on the language of the descendants of enslaved Niger-Congo Africans. In spite of the fact that well-known organizations, i.e., the Linguistic Society of America and the Board of Directors of Teachers of English to Speakers of Other Languages (TESOL), have recognized the speech and language of Black children as being a rule-governed linguistic system, with its own phonetic, phonological, morphological, semantic, and syntactic patterns, these same organizations are resistant when it comes to declaring that this language is an African language system that is, language-wise, genetically, unrelated to English (Crawford, 2001; Ramirez, et al., 2000). Even though these organizations and others declare that "numerous scientific studies over the past thirty years" have established the legitimacy of the language spoken by the parents of Black children and the children, they still falter when it comes to declaring it to be anything other than a dialect of English (Smith, 1998).

Dr. Ernie A. Smith, linguist, allowed the following excerpt to be reprinted in this Book from his unpublished article, "The Birth and Authentic Meaning of the Term Ebonics" (Smith, 2003). Hopefully, the reader will gain a better understanding of the term Ebonics after reading the excerpt :

> Despite the fact that the term Ebonics was coined and officially defined by African American scholars in 1973, the word Ebonics did not appear in any dictionary of the English language before 1997. In the 1998 edition of the *Oxford Dictionary of the English Language*, the word Ebonics appears. Rather than acknowledge the African origin of the idea, i.e., the original authorship of the term by an African American scholar, and provide the authentic meaning of the word Ebonics, the lexicographers of the *Oxford Dictionary* have elected to aid and abet the white supremacists' agenda. In the 1998 edition of the *Oxford Dictionary*, the word Ebonics is defined as:

Ebonics /eeboniks/ *n. pl.* the English used by black Americans, regarded as a language in its own right. (1991 p.258)

Notice, there is no acknowledgement of the original authorship of the term Ebonics by Dr. Robert Williams, and the definition is not the definition Dr. Robert Williams originally and officially declared. In the 1999 edition of Microsoft's *ENCARTA World English Dictionary*, the word Ebonics appears, also. Here, too, rather than acknowledge the original authorship of the term and the authentic meaning of the word Ebonics, the lexicographers of Microsoft's *ENCARTA World English Dictionary* have, likewise, elected to engage in literary theft of Dr. Robert Williams' original idea (i.e., the word Ebonics). I maintain that, in propagating a fraudulent definition of the term with the intent to deceive, the lexicographers of Microsoft's *ENCARTA World English Dictionary* engage in counterfeiting as well. Microsoft's *ENCARTA World English Dictionary* defines the word Ebonics as:

E-bon-nics /ee bonniks/ *n.* Black American English considered a language in its own right. The most scholars prefer the term AAVE (African American Vernacular English). (1999, p. 565)

Notice that, here again, there is no acknowledgement of the original authorship of the term Ebonics by Dr. Robert Williams, and here, too, the definition is not the definition that Dr. Robert Williams originally and officially declared. In *Merriam Webster's College Dictionary Tenth Edition* (2001), even after admitting the year 1973 was the year the word Ebonics first entered the English language, the word Ebonics is defined as follows:

> **Ebonics** \e-'ba-niks, i -, e-\ *n. pl but sing in constr* [blend of *ebony* and *phonics* 1973):
> BLACK ENGLISH (2001, p. 363)

Although *Merriam Webster's College Dictionary* does at least have the year the term Ebonics was coined correct, as in the case of the *Oxford Dictionary* and Microsoft's *ENCARTA Dictionary, Merriam Webster's Dictionary* does not acknowledge the original authorship of the term Ebonics or the definition originally and officially declared by Dr. Robert Williams. In the 2001 edition of the *Random House Webster's College Dictionary*, the word Ebonics appears. In the *Random House Webster's College Dictionary* the term Ebonics is defined as:

> **Ebonics** or **ebonics** (i bon'iks), n. (*used with a sing v.*) Black English [1970-1975, *Amer.*; b. of EBONY PHONICS]. (2001, p. 416)

In the *Random House Webster's College Dictionary*, the years 1970-1975 appear as the unspecified years that the word Ebonics entered into the English vocabulary. While the year 1975 at least concurs with the year that the book, *Ebonics: The True Language of Black Folk* (1975) was published, here, too, in lock step with the lexicographers of the *Oxford*, *ENCARTA*, and Merriam Webster's dictionaries, the *Random House Webster's College Dictionary* does not acknowledge the true authorship of the term Ebonics by Dr. Robert Williams. Likewise, in lock step with the lexicographers of the *Oxford*, *ENCARTA*, and Merriam Webster's Dictionaries, the *Random House Webster's College Dictionary* does not acknowledge the authentic meaning of the term Ebonics that Dr. Williams officially declared. But rather, the lexicographers of the *Random House Webster's College Dictionary* have also elected to engage in literary theft.

The refusal of the lexicographers of the English language dictionaries to acknowledge the original authorship of the term Ebonics by Dr. Robert Williams, and the official definition that was declared by him when the term was coined, is easy to explain. The basic premise of all white supremacists is that African people are sub-human. As such, in the white supremacist's view, African people have no innate capacity for language. That is, to have a language one has to have a thought. Since, in the white supremacist's view, Africans do not have the capacity to think, African people have never had an African language. This premise is at the core of the Black English (BE) and African American Vernacular English (AAVE) paradigm.

The Oakland Unified School District's resolution on Ebonics rocked the white supremacists' world. The white supremacists lexicographers' first tactic was a suppression of the truth by an outright refusal to even place the word Ebonics in their English language dictionaries. The second tactic of the white supremacists has been a suppression of the truth by entering the word Ebonics into their dictionaries, but propagating a fraudulent definition. Well, just as their first tactic of refusing to even place the word Ebonics into their dictionaries failed, their pathetic attempt to suppress the truth by entering the word Ebonics into their dictionaries and propagating a fraudulent definition, will meet with an even more resounding defeat. It is because the white supremacists cannot defend their position with empirical evidence and logical reasoning that they have resorted to this tactic, and the deviousness in which they elect to engage.

Merriam Webster's Collegiate Dictionary, Tenth Edition defines the word 'plagiarize' as follows:

> **plagiarize** \plā - jə - rīz\ to steal and pass off (the ideas or words of another) as one's own: use (a created production) without crediting the source ~ vi to commit literary theft: present as new and original an idea or product derived from an existing source − plagiarizer. (1993, p. 888)

Merriam Webster's Collegiate Dictionary, Tenth Edition defines the word 'counterfeit' as follows:

> **counterfeit** \ kaunt - ər -, fit\ 1. made in imitation of something else with intent to deceive . . . to try to deceive by pretense or dissembling. (1993, p. 265)

I maintain that, since "to steal and pass off the ideas or words of another as one's own" is 'plagiarism', and since a person who uses a "created production without crediting the source" commits literary theft, or plagiarism, when use is made of the term Ebonics (an original idea and word coined by Dr. Robert Williams) as a synonym for Black English, such usage is patently fraudulent. In as much as those who use the term Ebonics as a synonym for BE, NE, NNE, BVE, AAE, or AAVE, and do so with the intent to deceive, they are not only "plagiarizers", i.e., 'literary thieves', they are 'counterfeiters' as well. In summary, I maintain that the only authentic meaning of the term Ebonics is the definition that was declared in 1973 by Dr. Robert Williams.

Thus, the issue is not whether Ebonics is a 'language' or a 'dialect'. There are no languages that do not have dialects. The real issue is whether the preponderance of the empirical evidence supports the thesis that the language of descendants of enslaved Niger-Congo Africans is a dialect of English, and, hence, genetically akin to the Germanic language family to which English belongs. I maintain that the preponderance of the empirical evidence supports the thesis that the language of descendants of enslaved Niger-Congo Africans is the linguistic continuation of Africa in the diaspora, and, as such, is genetically akin to the Niger-Congo African language family. Put simply, **there is a difference between 'talking about the same thing and calling it something different' and 'talking about something different and calling it the same thing'.** The genesis of the grammar in the substratum of the language of descendants of enslaved Africans being the languages of Africa, the term Ebonics does not refer to a Black dialect of English. The term Ebonics refers to a neo-African language that is a dialect of the Niger-Congo African system. (Smith, 2003, unpublished manuscript)

Dr. Smith has spoken: This is a most vital and important subject that has a day of reckoning approaching.

1

EBONICS: THE PIDGIN-CREOLE THEORY

Ernie A. Smith, Ph.D.

The pidgin creole theory on the origin and historical development of the language of the descendants of enslaved Africans is rooted in a debate that emerged among sociologists, ethnologists and speech and language scholars known as Dialectologists and Pidgin/Creolists. In this debate we find, in the literature of the Dialectologists, Africans depicted as being primitive, dimwitted and docile savages who had not evolved successfully. In the Dialectologists' view, African people did not possess the higher order cortical capacity for fully human thoughts. Lacking the higher order cortical capacity for fully human thoughts, the Dialectologists posited Africans as having developed no fully human language system of their own. Unlike the Dialectologists, the Pidgin Creolists viewed Africans as human beings. Therefore, the Pidgin Creolists viewed Africans as people who did possess the cortical capacity for fully human thoughts and, as such, fully human language systems of their own.

In the literature of the Dialectologists, the depiction of the antebellum contacts between Europeans and enslaved Africans were depictions in which Africans had only the rudiments of a language with which to start. In the Dialectologists' view, the crude distress signals, mating calls and feral grunts that Africans did possess most certainly could not have been the grammatical or the lexical base upon which a two way communication system between the Europeans and enslaved Africans was developed. The Dialectologists' view is that, originally, the enslaved Africans had no competence whatsoever in the European languages to which they were exposed. Because the enslaved Africans had no competence in the language of their European captors or slave-masters, the Dialectologists posited it was incumbent upon the European slave-masters to devise a communication system in order to communicate with their African captives. According to the Dialectologists, this was done by Europeans having greatly "simplified" or "mutilated" their European speech. This greatly simplified European speech is depicted as being a form of speech comparable to that used by adults when they talk to "babies". Hence, what the Dialectologists put forth became known as the "baby talk" theory.

It is this "baby talk", a "dummied down", "simplified", "corrupt", or "mutilated" form of the European language that was taught to the enslaved Africans, who then adopted the "baby talk" and made it their native tongue. This is precisely the view that was held and explicitly put forth by Professor George Phillip Krapp of Columbia University, the godfather of modern Dialectologists, who are proponents of the African American Vernacular English (AAVE) thesis.

Even though Professor Krapp conceded there was scant evidence to support his "baby talk" hypothesis, Professor Krapp posited the condition of dominance and subordination as being crucial in the creation of the English based plantation dialects. Inferring that Africans were docile tabula rasae or "blank slates" upon which the Europeans imprinted their infantile-like linguistic creations, in his book, *The English of the Negro*, G.P. Krapp (1924) describes the assimilation process as follows:

> The assimilation of the language of the Negroes to the whites did not take place all at once. Though the historical evidence is not as full as might be wished, the stages can be followed with some certainty. When the Negroes were first brought to America they could have known no English. Their usefulness as servants, however, required that some kind of communication between master and

slave should be developed. There is little likelihood that any masters exerted themselves to understand or to acquire the native language of the Negroes in order to communicate with them. On the contrary, from the very beginning the white overlords addressed themselves in English to their Black vassals. It is not difficult to imagine the kind of English this would be. It would be a very much simplified English - the kind of English some people employ when they talk to babies. (pp. 192-193)

Further evidence of the denigrating and demeaning view of African people held by the Dialectologists is found in the work of the Latino Dialectologist, Ambrose Gonzales. While he did not explicitly characterize Africans as being savages or feral beasts, clearly a Latino of the white supremacists ilk, in his work *Black Border* (1922), Gonzales belittles Africans as being biophysically unequipped to speak European languages. Gonzales states:

Slovenly and careless of speech, these Gullahs seized upon the peasant English used by some of the early settlers and by the white servants of the wealthier colonists, wrapped their clumsy tongues about it as well as they could, and, enriched with certain expressive African words, it issued through their flat noses and thick lips as so workable a form of speech that it was gradually adopted by the other slaves and became in time the accepted Negro speech of the lower districts of South Carolina and Georgia. The words are of course not African, for the African brought over or retained only a few words of his jungle tongue, and even these few are by no means authenticated as part of the original scant baggage of the Negro slaves. (p. 10)

This Latino Dialectologist is clearly of the more rabid and invective ilk in expressing his views regarding the oropharyngeal linguistic capacity of African people. In further demeaning and denigrating African people, Gonzales goes on to state:

> What became of this jungle speech? Why so few words should have survived is mystery, for even after freedom, a few native Africans of later importations were still living on the Carolina coast, and the old family servants often spoke, during and after the war, of native Africans they had known; but while they repeated tales that came by word of mouth from the dark continent... they seem to have picked from the mouths of their African brothers not a single jungle-word for the enrichment of their own speech. (Gonzales, 1922, p. 10)

Actually, Gonzales's view, that the physiogamy or oropharyngeal anatomy of African people was not suited for speaking European languages, merely apes a similar denigration made earlier by another white supremacist Latino. In his work *Sons et Formes du Creoles dans les Antilles*, the French writer, Rene Payen-Bellisle, states (1894): "In order to understand the absence in French Creole dialects of the front rounded vowels of French, one merely had to look at the lips of the Negro" (Payen-Bellisle, 1894, p. 22). Here, in this quote of Rene Payen-Bellisle, we have an example of the profound scholarship that undergirds the Dialectologists' "baby talk" theory. Because the Dialectologists viewed Africans as savages that did not have fully developed languages, studying the primal grunts and semi-savage gibberish of the African people was deemed to be absurd. Uniform in their belief that the enslaved Africans in America lost what scant baggage of a language they possessed, in Africa, the Dialectologists posited the influence of **Early Modern English** (EModE) spoken by peasant British settlers as a major contributor, and the essence of the differences found in the dialect of enslaved Africans. In his book *Africanisms in the Gullah Dialect* (1949), concerning British Dialects and Baby-Talk, Lorenzo Turner states:

> Many Americans who have attempted to explain Gullah have greatly underestimated the extent of the African element in this strange dialect. Observing many characteristics that Gullah has in common with certain British dialects of the seventeenth and eighteenth centuries, they have not considered it necessary to acquaint themselves with any of the languages spoken in those sections of west Africa from which the Negroes were brought to the New World as slaves, nor to study the speech of the Negroes in those parts of the New World where English is not spoken; but rather have they taken the position that British dialects offer a satisfactory solution to all the problems presented by Gullah. They contend also that Gullah is partly a survival of baby-talk which the white people, during the early period of slavery, found it necessary to use in communicating with the slaves. (p. 5)

Clearly, the Dialectologists' view was that, from the very inception of the colonial era contacts between the Niger-Congo African and the European people, the hybrid vernaculars that emerged, for purposes of trading and other transactions between the Europeans and Africans, were the unique linguistic inventions and creations of the Europeans. Where the English language was concerned, the Dialectologists' view was that the English language was not only the dominant vocabulary in the hybrid vernacular of the enslaved Africans, in their view, EModE "baby-talk" was, in fact, the base of the grammar rules that underlies the deep phonetic, phonology, morphology and syntax of the enslaved Africans' corrupt English. The Dialectologists' view was that, if there are any African elements in the speech of the descendants of enslaved

Africans, they are not linguistic retentions made by Africans. According to the Dialectologists, any African elements in AAVE are "borrowings" made by EModE speaking British settlers from the African's "jungle gibberish". In other words, with the exception of a scant few jungle words here and there, the African features in AAVE are features adopted by the EModE speaking British slave masters and peasants, who then assimilated the African features into a corrupt or a mutilated form of EModE "baby talk". The Dialectologists contend that the British slave masters and peasants then re-introduced the African features to the enslaved Africans via the "baby talk" that the British slave masters and peasants created and taught to the enslaved Africans.

In essence, the Dialectologists' view is that, in the AAVE of descendants of enslaved Africans, there are no African grammatical elements or features that are African linguistic features that were retained by the enslaved Africans and transmitted to their descendants at all. Simply put, whereas the Dialectologists viewed and depicted African people as being jungle savages that were too mentally infantile to comprehend the commonly used speech spoken by colonial European adults, the Pidgin/Creolists were more disposed to viewing Africans as human beings. Being also more scientifically inclined, as their explanation of the linguistic hybridization process, the Pidgin/Creolists posited a linguistic fusion in which a mixed vernacular or dialect emerged that was a blending of both the African and European languages. According to the Pidgin/Creolists, this blended vernacular that facilitated communications between the Africans and the Europeans was a common language that served as a LINGUA FRANCA [1]. According

---

[1]LINGUA FRANCA is a language used for purposes of wider communication, especially in a group when the native language of no member of the group will suffice. If a Puerto Rican, a German, an Israeli, and an Icelander speak to each other in English, then English is being used as a lingua franca. The Mediterranean *lingua franca* known as Sabir was an outstanding example of such a language. A *lingua franca* which has no native speakers (like Sabir, but unlike English) is a PIDGIN (q.v.)." (See Dillard, 1972, p. 302).

to David DeCamp, unlike the Dialectologists, it was a Pidgin/Creolist, Leonard Bloomfield, who at least attempted to rationally explain the "baby talk" theory. DeCamp (1977) states:

> Bloomfield (1933:72-5) most fully developed the baby talk theory. Seeing in the process of pidgin creation a recursive series of imitations; i.e., the standard English speaker would contemptuously imitate the native's 'desperate attempt' to imitate the standard English. The native would then imitate the imitation of his imitation, and so on. (p. 19)

While Bloomfield and several other Pidgin/Creolists scholars attempted to, rationally, explain the "baby talk" theory, there were others that outright rejected the "baby talk" theory as incredibly naïve and simplistic. In his criticism and rejection of the "baby talk" theory, David DeCamp (1977) states:

> The baby-talk theory is easily refuted. First, all the early accounts (dating from the eighteenth century in Jamaica, for example) report that the white planters and their families were learning the creole from the slaves, not vice versa (Cassidy 1961, pp. 21-3). Furthermore, if each European had indeed improvised his own variety of baby-talk to communicate with his servants and slaves, how could one explain the fact that all dialects of creole French, including those in the Indian Ocean, are mutually intelligible? The typological similarities shared by creole French, English, Spanish, etc., are too great for coincidence, and when we consider that these creoles also share many common vocabulary words, including syntactic function words, the baby-talk hypothesis completely collapses. (p. 19)

In the discussion of the Pidgin-Creole theory thus far, the terms "pidgin" and "creole" have been used without any explicit definition or precise meaning being given. This prompts the question, what precisely is the meaning of the words "pidgin" and "creole"? In the glossary of his book, *Black English: Its History and Usage in the United States*, Joseph Dillard (1973) states:

> PIDGIN refers to a language which has no native speakers. It thus exists only as a LINGUA FRANCA (q.v.) When the pidgin becomes the only language of a speech community it then becomes a CREOLE (q.v.). (p. 303)

In an article entitled "The Study of Pidgin and Creole Languages", David DeCamp provides an etymological origin and a more detailed definition of the word "pidgin". DeCamp (1977) states:

> The traditional etymology derives *pidgin* from English *business*, and indeed expressions like 'That's my pigeon!' (i.e. that's my own private affair) are still common in Sino-English. Although the etymology has been challenged (Kleinecke 1959; cf. Hall, 1966, p. 7), the word in this sense was first applied to Chinese pidgin English, and later to any language of similar type. A pidgin is a contact vernacular, normally not the native language of any of its speakers. It is used in trading or in any situation requiring communication between persons who do not speak each other's native languages. (See DeCamp in Dell Hymes' *Pidginization and Creolization of Languages*, 1977, p. 15)

As the definition of the word "creole", in the glossary of his book, *Black English*, Joseph Dillard (1973) states:

CREOLE, in linguistic usage, refers to a language which was a PIDGIN (q.v.) at an earlier historical stage, but which became the only (or principal) language of a speech community. The best known creoles are Haitian (French) Creole and Sranan Tongo of Surinam. There are related creole languages in West Africa and in the Pacific. (p. 300)

In his article "The Study of Pidgin and Creole Languages" (1977), David DeCamp provides the following as an etymology and definition of the word "creole". He states:

The term *creole* (from the Portuguese *crioulo*, via Spanish and French) originally meant a white man of European descent born and raised in a tropical or semi-tropical colony. Only later was the meaning extended to include indigenous natives and others of non-European origin, e.g. African slaves. The term was then applied to certain languages spoken by creoles in and around the Caribbean and in West Africa and was later extended to other languages of similar types. (See DeCamp in Dell Hymes' *Pidginization and Creolization of Languages*, p. 15.)

A critical examination of contemporary Pidgin/Creolists literature reveals that, although the Pidgin/Creolists view some non-European, i.e., Arabic and Berber, and African mixed dialects as being African language based, conspicuously, all Pidgin/Creolists posit the African and European mixed or hybrid dialects that emerged from the convergence of the African and European languages as being European language based. However, on the issue of which particular European 'language family' all European pidgin creoles were originally based, the Pidgin/Creolists are divided into two camps: those who posit a "Polygenesis" view and those who posit a "Monogenesis" view.

THE POLYGENESIS VIEW

The Pidgin/Creolists who posit the polygenesis view are those who view the world's pidgin and creole dialects as having been created independently by each of the European language speaking nations that settled in the African, Asian, the Caribbean and the Latin American diaspora. The polygenecists contend that, in the beginning, as primarily a lingua franca used for trading interactions, in the Portuguese colonies there emerged a Portuguese Pidgin. In the Spanish colonies there emerged a Spanish Pidgin, and in the Dutch, French and English colonies, a Dutch, French, and English Pidgin emerged, respectively.

According to the polygenecists, as time passed and the slave trade flourished on the West coast of Africa, in the Caribbean, and in the colonial North and South American diaspora, many descendants of enslaved Africans were born into colonial European dominated social environments. The polygenecists contend that it was in these European dominated social environments that the transactional lingua francas or plantation pidgin dialects were developed and acquired by Africans as their native languages or mother tongues. The view of the polygenecists is that, over time, in the new world colonies or diaspora, the pidgin vernaculars that were initially created on the West coast of Africa for trading and other transactions became the principle vehicle for communication between the captive Africans and their European slave-masters. The polygenecists contend that, being born in captivity and exposed only to a plantation pidgin dialect, enslaved Africans acquired these hybrid pidgins or contact vernaculars as their primary languages or mother tongues. As stated earlier above, it is when pidgin dialects are acquired as an enslaved African's primary language or mother tongue that their language is distinguished as being a Creole language. Thus, the polygenesist's view is that, in Dutch Colonies, Dutch pidgin became a Dutch creole; in English colonies, English pidgin became an English creole; in French colonies, French pidgin became a French creole, and in the Portuguese and Spanish colonies, Portuguese and Spanish pidgins became Portuguese and Spanish creoles, respectively. However, as I have stated above, not all Pidgin/Creolists subscribe to the theory that each of the new world "pidgin" and subsequent "creole" dialects were the language specific creations of each colonial European speech community wherein they emerged.

The Pidgin/Creolists contend that the language of descendants of enslaved Africans in the United States has undergone a third stage in its development, and has become a full-fledged social dialect of English (the Gullah dialect being an exception). This third stage is described in the Pidgin/Creolists' literature as a process called de-creolization. According to the Pidgin/Creolists, it is in this de-creolized stage that a complete linguistic assimilation occurs, and the language of enslaved Africans is posited as having become so completely Anglicized and assimilated that it is now a mere non-standard social dialect or African American Vernacular of English (AAVE). [See the definition of creolization and decreolization in Crystal's *Dictionary of Linguistic and Phonetics* (1997, p. 99).]

In the contemporary Pidgin/Creolists' literature, we find that all Pidgin/Creolists uniformly view the language of the descendants of enslaved Africans in America as being a dialect of English. As evidence of this uniformity of opinion among Pidgin/Creolists, I cite the Memorandum Opinion and Order issued by the Judge Charles Joiner of the U.S. Federal District Court in Ann Arbor Michigan, *(Martin Luther King Junior Elementary School Children, et al. vs. Ann Arbor School District Board*, 1979). Judge Joiner states:

> The issue before this court is whether the defendant School Board has violated Section 1703(f) of Title 20 of the United States Code as its actions relate to the 11 black children who are plaintiffs in this case and who are students in the Martin Luther King Jr. Elementary School operated by the defendant School Board. It is alleged that the children

speak a version of "black English," "black vernacular" or "black dialect" as their home and community language that impedes their equal participation in the instructional programs, and that the school has not taken appropriate action to overcome the barrier. (pp. 1-2)

The view of the parents of the eleven Black children in the Ann Arbor case is entirely different from the view of the parents of Black children in the 1996 Oakland Unified School District (OUSD) 'Ebonics' controversy. In the Ann Arbor case, the parents of the eleven children had identified the home language of their children as "black English", "black vernacular" or "black dialect". In the 1996 OUSD 'Ebonics' controversy, on the OUSD home language identification forms, the parents had identified "Ebonics", or "Pan African Language" as the home and primary language of their children. In his Memorandum Opinion and Order Judge Joiner (1979) goes on to state:

All of the distinguished researchers and professionals testified as to the existence of a language system, which is a part of the English language but different from the standard English used in the school setting, the commercial world, the world of the arts and sciences, among the professions and in government. It is and has been used at some time by 80% of the black people of this country and has as its genesis the transactional or pidgin language of slaves, which after a generation or two became a Creole language. Since then it has constantly been refined and brought closer to the standard as blacks have been brought closer to the mainstream of Society. (p. 13)

Notice that Judge Joiner said **"all"** of the experts testified that the very "genesis" of the language system called "black English" or "black

27

vernacular" was "**the transactional or pidgin language of slaves**". I maintain that the failure of the attorneys for the Ann Arbor School Board to offer an alternative scientific interpretation of the origin and historical development of the language of enslaved Africans in America compelled an opinion and ruling by the Federal Court in Ann Arbor that was based on junk science. By this I mean to be 'admissible' in civil and criminal proceedings, all scientific evidence must meet the Frye Test. The Frye Test refers to a standard for admission of scientific evidence at trial. It derives from a 1923 case, *U. S. v Frye*, 293 F. 1013 (D.C. Cir. 1923), in which the defendant offered the results of a lie detector test that he claimed demonstrated that he was telling the truth when he denied killing the victim. The court ruled that the evidence was inadmissible because the scientific principle upon which the procedure was based had not been "sufficiently established to have gained general acceptance in the particular field in which it belongs".

The fundamental incongruence in the pidgin creole theory, and the reason it has not gained general acceptance in the particular field in which it belongs, is that the pidgin creole theory is an oxymoronic contradiction. That is, in the science of linguistics, lexical or vocabulary affiliation is not the accepted scientific principle upon which language family kinship is determined. Yet, the Pidgin/Creolists posit the language of the descendants of enslaved Africans in America as being a dialect of English based solely on a shared vocabulary or lexical affiliation. This matter will be discussed in more detail below. For now, suffice it to say, given the fact that the Pidgin/Creolists' parent language lexifier theory has not gained general acceptance in the particular field in which it belongs, the pidgin creole theory actually does not meet the Kelly Frye general acceptance test as admissible scientific evidence.

In *The American Heritage Dictionary of the English Language* (1984, p. 1423) the following is posited as the etymology of the word vernacular: "**ver-nac-u-lar** [From Latin *vernāculus*, domestic from *verna*, native slave, probably from *Etruscan.]". In *Webster's Collegiate Dictionary Tenth*

Edition (2001) the following etymology and definition of the word "vernacular" is given as:

> **vernacular** \və (r)-ʻnak-yə-lar\ *adj* [L *vernaculus* native,
> **fr** *verna* slave born in his master's house, native] (1601) **1**
> **a:** using a language or dialect native to a region or country
> rather than a literary, cultured or foreign language **b:** of
> relating to, or being a nonstandard language or dialect of
> a place, region or country **c:** of, relating to, or being the
> normal spoken form of a language]. (p. 1308)

Note that the Latin etymon for the word "vernacular" is *vernaculus*. In Latin, the word *vernaculus* means; "native". The etymon *vernaculus* is from the Latin word *verna*. In Latin the word *verna* means "slave born in his master's house". In view of the original Latin meaning of the word, "**vernacular**", i.e., "slave born in his master's house", based on the original Latin meaning of the word *verna*, I maintain that the contemporary meaning of the word "**vernacular**" in the appellation AAVE, as the language of enslaved Africans in America, is clearly a "dog whistle" for the slur "language or vernacular of slaves born in the master's house".

Thus, as shown above, it was the Pidgin/Creolists' pidginization, creolization and de-creolization process that was presented to the U.S. Federal court in Ann Arbor, Michigan in 1979. Due to the fact that the attorneys for the Ann Arbor School Board failed to offer an alternative, scientific interpretation to the pidginization, creolization and de-creolization theory on the origin and historical development of Black American speech, the Pidgin/Creolists' pidginization, creolization and de-creolization theory was the only view offered to the Ann Arbor Federal Court. Because the pidginization, creolization and de-creolization theory seemed to be a very rational, cogent and plausible theory, the Ann Arbor Federal court accepted the pidgin/creole theory as a scientifically authentic theory. As a consequence, vested with a court decision veneer that it is a scientifically authentic theory, the pidgin/creole theory is the most publicized and is deceptively propagated as the only valid theory on the origin and historical development of Black American speech.

THE MONOGENESIS VIEW

The Pidgin/Creolists who posit the monogenesis view contend that European and non-Indo-European linguistic convergence and hybridization did not begin in the colonial or antebellum era. The proponents of the monogenesis view contend the historical evidence is that there were Indo-European contacts with non-Indo-European people many centuries earlier. In light of this historical fact, those who posit the monogenesis view contend that linguistic hybridization occurred when the first sustained contact was made between European and non-European people in Africa, the Far East and the South Pacific. Emphasizing the tremendous similarities that exist among the Caribbean creoles, and the parallel features that exist in the creoles of Asia and the South Pacific, the proponents of the monogenesis view contend that all pidgin/creoles have a common ancestor from which all pidgin and creole dialects have been formed. But then the proponents of the monogenesis view do not agree on, precisely, which ancestor Indo-European language the original proto-pidgin dialect was based. According to David DeCamp (1977):

> During the 1950's several scholars became increasingly dissatisfied with the polygenetic theories. In 1951 Navarro Tomas argued that Papiamento was not an indigenous Caribbean blend of Portuguese and/or Spanish with African elements, but rather had its origin in the Portuguese pidgin used as a trade jargon in West Africa during the slave trade. He was by no means the first to point out the key importance of Portuguese in the

history of pidgin-creole. Schuchardt had stressed the role of Portuguese, and Hesselings had seen it as the origin of both Afrikaans and Negerhollands. (See Dell Hymes' *Pidginization and Creolization of Languages*, 1977, p. 22)

Unlike the polygenecists (i.e., Bloomfield et al.) that attempted to uphold and rationally explain the "baby talk" theory, the proponents of the monogenesis view maintained that the blending or hybridization process that occurs to form a hybrid pidgin dialect is not a random or haphazard recursive series of imitations of a corrupted European standard language. But rather, the linguistic fusion or hybridization process is a very systematic synthesis that adheres to systematic rule governed principles. In this, the Pidgin/Creolists of both the monogenesis view and the polygenesis view are on one accord. In fact, other than the fact that they differ on whether all of the world's pidgin and creole dialects are grammatically derived from a single European linguistic base (Portuguese), the monogenecists and the polygenecists do not differ much at all. Describing the weaknesses of the monogenesis theory, David DeCamp (1977) states:

The supporters of monogenesis would thus have us think of Anglicized creole rather than creolized English. As yet, the theory rests on many assumptions and very little documentary evidence, but it has a great deal to recommend it...The weaknesses of the monogenetic theory are first a very sketchy historical documentation, second the controversial status of Far Eastern pidgin English (which lack many features shared by other pidgin and creoles) and third the problem of certain pidgins creoles which clearly developed without any direct Portuguese influence... (pp. 23-24)

Although they differ on the question of a single versus a multiple European language base for the world's pidgin and creole languages, as far as the linguistic convergence, transmission and hybridization process being a three staged pidginization, creolization and decreolization fusion of the African and European linguistic systems, the proponents of the monogenesis and the polygenesis views do not differ. As Pidgin/Creolists, whether the hybridization process entailed the restructuring of a European language or the relexification of an African language, both the monogenecists and polygenecists concur and posit a "reinforcement value of shared linguistic features" as the most plausible explanation for the identical characteristics that exists in the mixed pidgin speech of the enslaved Africans. DeCamp (1977) states:

> Even if we were to assume that the lexicon and the structure of a language were equally susceptible to change, relexification would still be a better explanation than restructuralization for the development of pidgins and creoles; for the influences which could bring about a wholesale adoption of French vocabulary in French territories, English vocabulary in British territories, etc., are clear and obvious, whereas there is no known sociolinguistic influence which could explain why the structures of five different European languages should have been modified in precisely the same direction. (pp. 23-24)

In essence, the "reinforcement value of shared or common linguistic features" that already existed in both the African and the European languages prior to any contact was that, when the African and the European languages converged, it was the prior existing features that both language systems already possessed that were the easiest to utilize. As such, the features that both languages possessed, prior to any contact, were the features that were retained and used in the hybridization process. Naturally, the existing features in both languages that were different presented the most difficulty.

According to the proponents of the monogenesis view, in the hybridization process, the features that were different or unalike, prior to any contact, were not utilized. This process of linguistic "hybridization" or "assimilation", via the utilization and "reinforcement of prior existing features" that both languages already had in common, and the rejection of uncommon or unalike features, was seen by the Pidgin/Creolists as being a very systematic method by which the speakers of EModE created what is currently called AAVE. The Pidgin/Creolists argued that two critical factors supported their thesis: (1) The evidence that much of what is considered to be uniquely different about Black American speech can, actually, be traced to EModE. (2) In the colonial diaspora the proportional population ratios of Europeans to enslaved Africans made the influence of EModE dominant.

When considered in the light of some very basic science principles, the Pidgin/Creolists thesis of hybridization and assimilation appears to be valid. That is, as a linguistic fusion or hybridization process that adheres to rule governed principles, the Pidgin/Creolists posited the linguistic fusion or hybridization process as being analogous to the well-known fusion or bonding principle that occurs in the science of chemistry.

According to Callewart and Genyea's text, *Basic Chemistry* (1980), J. Dudley Herron's text, *Understanding Chemistry* (1981), and Kotz and Purnell's text, *Chemistry & Chemical Reactivity* (1987), in chemistry, it is well known that 'all atoms seek to have a stable eight or two electrons in their outside shell (the octet rule). To achieve a stable octet (8), when atoms of low ionization energy encounter atoms of high electronegativity, atoms that have low ionization energies lose their electrons. Or rather, it is easiest to give them up. In losing their electrons these atoms end up with more protons than electrons and take a positive charge. Conversely, atoms with high ionization energies, i.e., atoms that have more electrons than protons, have a negative charge. When atoms of low ionization energy (those wanting to get rid of an electron) encounter atoms of high electronegativity (those wanting more electrons) there is a transfer of electrons from one to the other. This forms both a positive ion and a negative ion. The attractive force of these opposite charges holds the atoms together in an IONIC BOND[2]. On the other hand, "when two atoms with the same electron affinity encounter each other, there can't be a transfer of electrons. When this occurs, because both atoms want the electron – or electrons with EQUAL force, "a bond is formed between two atoms by the sharing of one or more electrons." When a bond is formed by two atoms sharing one or more electrons, this is called a "covalent bond"[3]. Unlike "ionic" bonding, in which "likes repel and un-alikes attract", in covalent bonding, "likes appear to attract and un-alikes appear to repel". However, actually, what occurs is that two "alikes" are attracted to the same "un-alike". Because neither atom can completely possess the electron, they both share it.

In sharing one or more electrons, each atom "thinks" that it is surrounded by eight electrons. (See also Study Guide Intro to Chemistry 110, Chaffey College).

It is this principle of "covalent" bonding around an atom shared in common to which the notion of linguistic blending or "hybridization" by the sharing of features already held in common, is analogous. The analogy is that, in the blending process, each language system bonds around the linguistic features that it "thinks" belongs to it. Also, in

---

2**Ionic Bond**: a chemical bond formed between oppositely charged species because of their mutual electrostatic attraction. [See Webster's Collegiate Dictionary Tenth Edition (1993, p. 618)]

3**Covalent bond:** A chemical bond formed when two ATOMS with the same electron AFFINITY are sharing the same outside or valance electrons. A nonionic chemical bond formed by shared electrons (*Webster's Seventh New Collegiate Dictionary* 1972, p. 192).

support of their "reinforcement value of shared features" the Pidgin/ Creolists cite a behavioral science reinforcement learning theory that they contend validates their view of the hybridization process.

Known in reinforcement learning theory as the "law of exercise", this principle holds that; the more an act is repeated, the more an act is reinforced and, hence, the act gets learned. The "law of exercise" also holds that, conversely, the less an act is repeated, the less it gets reinforced and, hence, the less it gets learned. In fact, the "law of exercise" holds that, acts frequently repeated tend to extinguish acts that are performed infrequently. In essence, the "law of exercise" operates on a principle of reinforcement called "operant conditioning". In reinforcement learning theory the meaning of the word "operant" is; "that which operates to produce an effect, i.e., a response or behavior elicited by an environment rather than a specific stimulus". The meaning of the word "conditioning" is; "conditioning in which the desired behavior or increasingly closer approximations to it are followed by a rewarding or reinforcing stimulus". (See *Webster's Collegiate Dictionary, Tenth Edition*, 2001, p. 813.)

As viewed by the early Pidgin/Creolists, "Black English" (BE), Black Vernacular English (BEV) or AAVE was invented by English speaking Europeans and taught to Africans through a "stimulus response" conditioning process. Although the "stimulus response", "law of exercise" thesis that the Pidgin/Creolists put forth appears to be a very coherent and cogent thesis, in learning theory, the principle that "the more an act is repeated the more it gets learned" is only valid in conjunction with another "conditioning" principle. That conditioning principle is known as the "law of effect". As a principle that explains <u>why</u> certain acts tend to get repeated while other acts do not, the "law of effect" holds that it is not repetition alone, or in and of itself, that causes an act to get repeated. It is "positive reinforcement" of the act. That is, as a rule, the acts that tend to get repeated are acts that gratify a basic want or need. Acts that are not gratifying, or acts that do not get gratified, tend not to get repeated and, hence, do not get learned. Needless to say, as an analogy to the linguistic blending or hybridization process, pivotal to the validity of the "law of exercise" and "law of effect" stimulus response reinforcement theory is whether or not there was "positive reinforcement". In essence, in order for the enslaved Africans to have been taught an EModE based pidgin dialect, the "social conditioning" interactions between the EModE speaking settlers and the enslaved Africans would have to have been contacts in which there was "positive reinforcement".

In support of their view, that the hybridization process and learning of the pidgin English by the enslaved Africans occurred as a function of "positive reinforcement", the Pidgin/Creolists posit a "proportional population ratios" and "dominance and subordination" thesis. The "proportional population ratios" and "dominance and subordination" thesis is that; in the antebellum era the EModE speaking settlers outnumbered the enslaved Africans. They contend that this numerical majority made the influence of the EModE language dominant in the hybridization process. However, the claim that the proportional population ratios of Europeans to enslaved Africans made the influence of EModE dominant, is contradicted by two critical facts. Firstly, according to the accounts given by most historians, there were far more enslaved Africans on plantations than Europeans [See Elkins (1971), Franklin (1980), Lynd (1967)].

Clearly, in terms of the extent to which the population ratio of Whites to Blacks influenced the hybridization process, if there were more enslaved Africans than EModE speaking settlers on the antebellum plantations, then based on population ratios, the language of the enslaved Africans would have been dominant in the hybridization process. Secondly, with regards to the social contacts and linguistic interactions between the enslaved Africans and the EModE speaking settlers, the contention of the Pidgin/Creolists does not square with the certain historical facts. One fact being, according to the vast majority of historians, cultural anthropologists, and sociologists, human enslavement is not normal, and plantation systems are not normal societies. The empirical evidence is that, for the enslaved Africans, conditions were very harsh, cruel and inhumane. In particular, in their attempts to reduce the enslaved Africans to the level of mute brutes, the EModE speaking Europeans used a host of measures to prevent any and all language use, development and learning among the enslaved Africans.

Another fact that refutes the Pidgin/Creolists' view of what the socio-linguistic conditions were on the antebellum plantations is that, according to the historians, cultural anthropologists and sociologists, there were far more conditions which were designed to impede normal language from emerging among the enslaved Africans and, thus, preventing any normal communications from developing between them. Most notably, there was a denial of formal European language and literacy instruction to enslaved Africans via anti-literacy laws. Also, to restrict speech among the enslaved Africans, another more vile and vicious measure employed by the British settlers and colonial plantation owners, to restrict and prevent the learning of the European languages, was the use of a harness or mouthpiece called a "bit". In a PBS televised interview, Pulitzer Prize winning author, Toni Morrison, describes how, as a means of punishing enslaved Africans who verbally "back sassed" or acted "uppity" towards ole massa, many enslaved Africans were compelled to wear a "bit" in their mouths. Although, as an explanation for this heinous practice many white supremacists posit that it was to prevent the slaves from eating up the crop, the record reveals that the "bit" was used primarily to prevent two way oral communication and, hence, conspiracies among the rebellious slaves (Morrison (1990).

I maintain that, just as use of the "bit" prevented conversations and conspiracies between the enslaved Africans, the "bit" also prevented two-way oral communications between the slave-master and the enslaved Africans compelled to wear them. There is also empirical evidence that, besides the "bit" as another means of circumventing slave rebellions, rather than physically mutilate and permanently maim their recalcitrant enslaved Africans, many planters found it much more profitable to just sell them off to other plantations. Needless to say, not all enslaved Africans who behaved belligerently were compelled to wear a "bit" or sold off. The historians report that to terrorize and instill fear in the enslaved African masses, many unruly enslaved Africans were publicly whipped and beaten to death.

Also, as evidence of what the social conditions were on the antebellum plantations, there is the well documented fact that, very often, as a measure to prevent conspiracies and insurrections, the enslaved Africans were segregated linguistically. Indeed, the Pidgin/Creolists cite the practice of segregating the enslaved Africans, linguistically, as the very means by which the enslaved Africans were "driven" to the use of the European invented pidgin vernaculars. There is incongruence in this Pidgin/Creolists assertion here. For, if in order to prevent conspiracies, the enslaved Africans were segregated, linguistically, and if it was via this linguistic segregation that the enslaved Africans were "driven" to the use of a common "pidgin" dialect, then the bitter irony is that the linguistic segregation did not prevent conspiracies or revolts. That is, as opposed to driving the enslaved Africans to use a common pidgin dialect and preventing communications between the enslaved Africans, the fact is the common pidgin dialect actually facilitated more effective communications between the enslaved Africans. Clearly, if the common pidgin dialect actually facilitated more effective communications between the enslaved Africans, then the common pidgin dialect, in fact, facilitated the enslaved Africans' conspiracies and, in effect, aided the enslaved Africans' insurrections and revolts.

The fact of the matter is historians report that it was mainly on the slave ships that, as a means of circumventing communication and organized revolts, the slaves were separated ethnically and linguistically. According to the historians, the records of activities at the slave auction and on the plantations reveal that, as a rule, the plantation owners did not follow this practice. In fact, in his book *Black English* Joseph Dillard (1973, p.74) states that, among the planters, just as people prefer certain breeds of cows, horses and dogs, the more common practice was that the plantation owners preferred and selected Africans from the same tribes or ethnic backgrounds.

Thus, the thesis that the "reinforcement of common linguistic features", the "proportional population ratios" and European "dominance" had the greater influence in the hybridization process is refuted by the empirical evidence that, as opposed to encouraging two way communications and reinforcing language development among the enslaved Africans, the actual social practice was more that of prohibiting enslaved Africans from talking period. In so far as encouraging two way communications between the enslaved Africans and the EModE speaking British slave masters, the empirical evidence is that, except for those enslaved Africans deemed to be more useful as house servants, there was little or no communications between the enslaved Africans and the slave-master at all.

The fact is, as opposed to purposefully teaching enslaved Africans the EModE of the British settlers and plantation owners, the actual social practice was more commonly the attempt to reduce the enslaved Africans to the level of mute brutes by prohibiting their EModE language development and literacy. The following are but a few of the measures and tactics employed by the EModE speaking British settlers and plantation owners, to prevent the enslaved Africans' communications and EModE literacy:

(1) the linguistic segregation of enslaved Africans;
(2) the use of anti-literacy laws, prohibiting the teaching of Africans to read and write;
(3) the fitting of "uppity" enslaved Africans with "bits";
(4) the practice of selling "belligerent" enslaved Africans off; and
(5) whipping "belligerent" enslaved Africans to death;

I maintain that all of these measures and tactics raise serious doubt as to whether any extensive oral communication between the enslaved Africans and their English speaking slave-masters even occurred. In other words, in my view, linguistically, the EModE speaking slave masters and other Europeans did not purposefully teach the enslaved Africans anything.

When Pidgin/Creolists are confronted with the empirical evidence that enslaved Africans actually outnumbered Europeans on the antebellum plantations, unable to sustain their claim of numerical dominance, the Pidgin/Creolists then attempt to negate the influence of numerical dominance by contending that it was not so much the dominant numerical population ratios, but rather the dominant social role of the Europeans over the Africans that determined the language base upon which the hybrid pidgin dialects were formed. When confronted with the fact that their social dominance thesis is refuted by the empirical evidence of a lack of any sustained master and enslaved African contacts that would have been positive reinforcement for language acquisition and development among the Africans, the Pidgin/Creolists resort to what they contend was a profoundly diffuse linguistic state of enslaved Africans from all parts of Africa as another subterfuge.

What the Pidgin/Creolists contend here is that the language diversity of Africa was so vast on the continent that, in any given African idiom, only a handful of Africans could even be found that could communicate with each other. The Pidgin/Creolists contend that this profound African linguistic diversity, combined with the practice of segregating enslaved Africans who spoke the same African languages, "drove" the enslaved Africans to the use of the European invented plantation pidgin dialects. However, I maintain that the fact is the segregation of the enslaved Africans linguistically did not "drive" the enslaved Africans to the use of a hybrid pidgin dialect invented by Europeans. It merely aided the enslaved African's adoption of the common European vocabulary. It was the already existing common Niger-Congo African grammar that facilitated the hybridization process that became what is known today as Ebonics.

While the existence of common or shared linguistic features in the African languages and the EModE of British settlers prior to any linguistic convergence was seen as a plausible explanation for the hybridization process by which the pidgin dialect of the enslaved Africans emerged, there were structural linguistic features in the pidgin dialect of the enslaved Africans that were not found in or traced to the EModE of the British settlers. The structural linguistic differences in the hybrid pidgin dialect of the enslaved Africans that were features not found in or traced to the EModE of the British settlers begged for an explanation and full accounting.

In an attempt to account for the structural linguistic features existing in the pidgin dialect of the enslaved Africans that were not the found in or traced to the EModE spoken by the British settlers, the early Pidgin/Creolists posited the unaccounted for differences as features introduced into the pidgin of the enslaved Africans by poor white Scots-Irish peasants who also, in order to communicate with the Africans, had to dummy down or greatly mutilate their Scots-Irish Celtic dialects. In an article entitled "The History of Black English" (1973), the Scots-Irish influence on the hybridization process of pidgin English of the enslaved African is described by the late Dr. Mary R. Key. In this article Key posits that the Scottish colonials owned many slaves and that on many plantations, owned by the EModE speaking British planters, the Scots were the principle drivers or foremen. Key posits that (as they are so prevalent as policemen and military servicemen today) the Scottish and Irish overseers had more contact with the enslaved Africans than the EModE speaking British owners of the plantations.

Thus, according to Key, the features in the grammar of Black English that cannot be traced to Old, Middle or EModE, are very likely traceable to the Old Irish and Old Ulster Scots dialects. She writes in "The History of Black English" (1973):

There are some indications the Scots dialect might have had a greater influence on the development of BE than has been previously recognized. The immigration of the Ulster Scots as well as the other Scottish pioneers paralleled the entrance of the Black people to the United States. History books tell of their close contact. Such as Scots foremen to slave workers...The possible close relationship of the Scots dialect and the development of BE is further hinted at by the frequent use of Scots or Gaelic names by Black people who had to adopt a surname for identification among English speakers. (pp. 3-4)

Of course, the extent to which enslaved Africans had more contact with the Scottish and Irish people than with the English would mean that many elements in the underlying grammar of Black American speech would more likely be traced to the Celtic language continuum than to the EModE. The incongruence in citing the plantation labor relationships and influence of the Ulster Scots and Irish dialects is that, in the case of Celtic features found in the pidgin dialects of enslaved Africans, many, if not most, of the Celtic features discerned were features that had already been adopted into EModE by the British. Unable to trace the vast majority of the differences in the grammar of the descendants of enslaved Africans to the EModE and Celtic dialects of the Scots and Irish, the early Pidgin/Creolists were still unable to account for the structural linguistic features existing in the pidgin dialect of the enslaved Africans. This compelled the early Pidgin/Creolists to more thoroughly examine the highly structured and rule governed features in the substratum of the hybrid pidgin dialects spoken by descendants of enslaved Africans. Predicated on their reinforcement value of shared or common linguistic features, the early Pidgin/Creolists were compelled to become even more familiar with the grammatical structure of the autochthonous African languages spoken on the African continent.

It is imperative and must be clearly understood that, while the Pidgin/Creolists did adopt the perspective that they should become more familiar with the grammatical structure of the autochthonous African languages spoken on the African continent, it was not the Pidgin/Creolists, but rather, the scholars and researchers in the fields of cultural anthropology and comparative linguistics, who did the seminal work that involved studying the autochthonous African languages and their grammatical structure. These scholars, commonly called "Africanists", whose primary interest and focus was on the autochthonous African languages, produced volumes of empirical evidence that, independent of the Indo-European languages, African languages had systematic, rule governed and predictable grammars of their own. In other words, it was the work of the Africanists that exploded the myth that African people were dim-witted savages that had not developed fully human languages of their own.

The empirical evidence, that African languages had systematic, rule governed and predictable grammars of their own, independent of EModE and other Indo-European languages, vindicated the Pidgin/Creolists in their rejection of the Dialectologists' "baby talk" theory. It was the empirical data on African language structures produced by the Africanist researchers in anthropology, structural and comparative linguistics that was the data base upon which the Pidgin/Creolists made their contrastive analysis of the African and EModE shared linguistic features. Hence, the data on African language structures produced by the Africanist researchers was the data source of the Pidgin/Creolist's reinforcement value of the common linguistic features thesis. Likewise, it was the data on the autochthonous African language structures produced by the Africanists that was the source upon which Pidgin/Creolists made their comparisons of the unexplained structural linguistic features in the pidgin dialect of the enslaved Africans.

When the Pidgin/Creolists compared the unexplained linguistic features in the pidgin dialect of the enslaved Africans with the structural linguistic features of the autochthonous African languages, applying the universally established scientific criterion of common origin and continuity of the rules of grammar as the criterion for positing kinship, they were compelled by the hard evidence to acknowledge that the grammar of the, so-called, pidgin creole dialects of the enslaved Africans were not EModE language based. Adhering to the criterion of common origin and continuity in the rules of grammar as the scientific principle for classifying and positing genetic kinship in languages, the Pidgin/Creolists were compelled to acknowledge the irrefutable empirical evidence, produced by the Africanists, that the grammar of the hybrid African and European dialects are African language based. But then, despite the fact that, on the basis of common origin and continuity in the rules of grammar, all African and European hybrid pidgin-creole dialects should be classified as African language based, there are no Pidgin/Creolists that posit the language of descendants of enslaved Africans in America as being the linguistic continuation of Africa in Black America. Attestation to my contention, that all Pidgin/Creolists view African and European pidgin/creole dialects as being European language based, is provided by David DeCamp. In his article "The Study of Pidgin and Creole Languages", DeCamp states:

> The terminology of pidgin-creole studies reflects the traditional classification and theory of origin of these languages. Each pidgin or creole has been traditionally classed as a deviant dialect of a standard language, usually European, with English, French, Portuguese, Spanish and Dutch the most frequent. A creole which shares most of its vocabulary with English is traditionally called an English-based creole or creolized English. Most creoles, like most pidgins, are European based, i.e. each has derived most of its vocabulary from one or more European languages. Creole French (also called *patois*)

and creole English are the most frequent in West Africa and the New World, but Spanish, Dutch, and Portuguese creoles are common in other parts of the world... (See DeCamp in Dell Hymes' *Pidginization and Creolization of Languages*, 1977, pp. 15 - 16)

Further attestation that the parent language lexifier is the criterion used by the Pidgin/Creolists as their basis for positing linguistic kinship, and that all Pidgin/Creolists view African and European pidgin creoles as being European language based", is provided by Suzanne Romaine. In her book, *Language in Society*, Romaine (1994) states:

Pidgin and creole languages are spoken mainly in Third World countries. Their role there is intimately connected with a variety of political and social questions. There are probably more than a hundred pidgin and creole languages in daily use around the world, and more speakers of these languages than there are of Swedish. The exact number is difficult to establish because it depends on how we define the term 'pidgin' and 'creole'... Most pidgins and creoles are based on European languages, in particular Spanish, Portuguese, French and English. However, those based on English are more numerous than those based on any other language, attesting to the greater spread of English than any other metropolitan language. The next largest group is based on French, and a much smaller number based on non-European languages, such as Sango spoken in the Central African Republic. (pp. 163-164)

Notice Romaine states that "most pidgins and creoles are based on European languages". This prompts the question what does the term "based" mean? Romaine (1994) states:

The term '-based' means that the bulk of the lexicon is drawn from that language, while the grammatical structure typically shows influence from other (usually non-European) languages. These other languages are referred to as the 'substrate'. Thus, when scholars speak of English based creoles, they are referring to all those creoles which have taken most of their vocabulary from English. Terms such as 'English lexicon' or 'English lexifier pidgin/creole' are also used and the lexifier language is sometimes called the 'superstrate'. While it has often been the case that scholars have treated English-based pidgin/creoles as dialects of English and French pidgin/creoles as Romance dialects, etc., most now recognize that creoles are languages in their own right with an independent structure. They are not parasitic systems or corrupted versions of the languages to which they are most closely related at the lexical level. (p. 164)

As I have stated earlier, the fundamental incongruence in the pidgin creole theory, and why it has not gained general acceptance in comparative linguistics (in the particular field in which it belongs) is that the pidgin creole theory is an oxymoronic contradiction. By this I mean, in the science of linguistics, it is universally understood and generally accepted that, it is based on common origins and continuity in the rules of grammar, that languages are classified and posited as being akin or genetically related. In fact, despite the fact that the bulk of the English lexicon or vocabulary has been adopted from Latin and French, it is based on common origins and continuity in the rules of grammar that English is, itself, classified and defined as a West Germanic language. As I have shown above, unable to deny that the grammar in the substratum of the pidgin dialects follows the rules of African grammar, and, therefore, unable to posit EModE and the Celtic languages as the grammatical base of the pidgin dialect of the enslaved Africans, the Pidgin/Creolists were left with only the vocabulary or lexicon adopted from the EModE and Celtic languages upon which they could even posit an affiliation. The English language posited as being the dominant European lexifier of AAVE, conveniently, the Pidgin/Creolists abandoned the universally established scientific criterion of common origin and continuity of the rules of grammar as their criterion for positing kinship. Positing, instead, an un-scientific, dominant lexifier theory as their criterion for language family kinship, in one fell swoop, the mixed African and European, so-called, pidgin/creole dialects in America are classified as English language based. I maintain that, when the Pidgin/Creolists abandon the diachronic and comparative linguistics criterion of common origin and continuity in the rules of grammar as their criterion for positing linguistic family kinship, and posit the language of the descendants of enslaved Africans in America as being a dialect of English, the Pidgin/Creolists are, in fact, in lock step with the Dialectologists' view.

And so, whereas the Dialectologists posit the differences in the speech of Black people and White people in America as being related to innate and cognitive deficits and biophysical defects in the oropharyngeal anatomy of African people, a review of the Pidgin/Creolists' literature reveals that the Pidgin/Creolists' view of African people is subtly just as unscientific. *The American Heritage Dictionary* (1984) defines the word **'English'** as:

> **Eng·lish** (ing'lish) *adj*. 1.a Of, pertaining to, derived from, or characteristic of England and its inhabitants. 1. The people of England collectively. Used with *the* 2. The West Germanic language of the English divided historically into Old English, Middle English, and Modern English and now spoken in the British Isles, the United States, and numerous other countries. (p. 433)

In the science of diachronic and comparative linguistics, it is common origin and continuity of the rules of grammar (i.e., phonology, morphology and morpho-syntax) that is the criteria and basis upon which language family kinship is scientifically determined. Likewise, in Indo-European linguistics, it is common origin and continuity of the rules of grammar that is the prevailing and generally accepted principle upon which language family kinship is determined. As such, it is common origin and continuity of the rules of grammar that is the basis upon which the English language is classified as being a West Germanic language. As corroboration that it is common origin and continuity of the rules of grammar that is the basis upon which the English language is classified as being a West Germanic language, I cite Leonard Palmer (1972) who, in his book *Descriptive and Comparative Linguistics*, states:

> We repeat, then, that observed resemblances between speech habits, given the principle of arbitrariness, force us to the conclusion of historical connectedness, by an unbroken chain of mimetic acts. This connectedness is what is understood by 'relationship'. In order to establish the fact of such a relationship our evidence must not consist entirely of points of vocabulary. For, ... words are often borrowed by one language from another as a result of cultural contact. Thus, English has borrowed words like *algebra* from Arabic sources. No one on that account will assert that English is related to the Semitic languages. What constitutes the most certain evidence of relationship is resemblances of grammatical structure, for languages retain the native structure even when their vocabularies have been swamped by foreign borrowings, such has been the case for English and Hittite. (pp. 22-23)

As corroboration that the classification of Indo-European languages is based on genetic classification, i.e., common origin and continuity of the rules of grammar, and that it is based on continuity of morphology that English is classified as a Germanic language, in an article entitled "Linguistic Continuity of Africa in the Caribbean", Dr. Mervyn Alleyne attests that the bulk of the English lexicon is not from the West Germanic language stock. Positing the Romance or Latin languages as the source of the bulk of the English lexicon, Alleyne (1971) states:

> The most prevalent view concerning the basis for genetic classification in Indo-European linguistics is that continuity of morphology constitutes the relevant evidence for positing genetic relationship. For example, there has been linguistic continuity in Western Europe in terms of the transmission of Latin morphology (in somewhat altered form) or by the transmission of Old Germanic morphology. This makes languages like French, Spanish, etc., genetically related to Latin, and German, Dutch, etc., genetically related to Old Germanic. It is generally accepted that there has been no rupture in the development or transmission process, although obviously there has been change. English itself is considered to be a continuation of Anglo-Saxon, although in fact the vocabulary is predominantly Romance or Latin. (pp. 125-126)

The most glaring incongruence in the pidgin/creole theory is that the Pidgin/Creolists adhere to the principle of "genetic classification", i.e., common origin and continuity in the rules of grammar, as the basis upon which the English language is classified as being a West Germanic language. Yet, the Pidgin/Creolists abandon this principle for positing linguistic kinship when they classify the language of the descendants of enslaved Africans. That is, even though the English language is classified as being a West Germanic language, based on the common origin and continuity of the rules of Anglo-Saxon German grammar, the Pidgin/Creolists classify the language of the descendants of enslaved Africans as being a dialect of English, predicated on their thesis that the English language is the base from which the bulk of the Black English or AAVE vocabulary, i.e., lexicon, is derived.

The Pidgin/Creolists' shift from the genetic classification criteria as the basis by which the English language is classified as being a West Germanic language, to the criterion of the language from which the bulk of the lexicon is derived when classifying the language of the descendants of enslaved Africans, is rendered even more incongruent when we consider the fact that the bulk of the English lexicon is not from the West Germanic language stock. Corroboration that the bulk of the English lexicon is not from the West Germanic language stock is found in McDougal and Littell's text, *Building English Skills* (1978) wherein they state:(1978) pp. 1-5):

> There are more than half a million words in the English language. Where do they all come from? We could give a quick answer to that question by saying that most of the words in English are "borrowed" from other languages… About A.D. 500, three tribes of people were living in northern Europe. They were the Angles, the Saxons, and Jutes. They spoke one of the West Germanic languages. Linguists call their language Anglo-Saxon. We can think of Anglo-Saxon as the beginning of the English we speak today. In fact, some of the words used in Anglo-Saxon are still used in English today. We call them native English words…At the beginning of this chapter we said that most English words have been borrowed from other languages. The rest are native English words. Of the half million words in English, only about 15 percent are native English words. (pp. 1-5)

The bulk of the English lexicon being, in fact, adopted from the Latin or Romance language family, even if we assume for argument sake that the language family from which the bulk of the vocabulary is derived is a valid criterion for positing language family kinship, in positing AAVE as being English language based, the Pidgin/Creolists have misclassified AAVE. That is, the English language being itself, lexically, Romance language based, then, AAVE is also, lexically, Romance language based. The bulk of the lexicon of AAVE, being, in fact, Romance language based, the Pidgin/Creolists dominant lexifier thesis collapses on its own criterion.

And so, I have examined and critically analyzed the Pidgin/Creolists' theory on the origin and historical development of the language of descendants of enslaved Niger-Congo Africans. I have established that, in comparative linguistics, it is common origin and continuity of the rules of grammar (i.e., phonology, morphology and morpho-syntax) that is the criteria and basis upon which language family kinship is scientifically determined. I have shown that, likewise, in Indo-European linguistics, it is common origin and continuity of the rules of grammar that is the prevailing and generally accepted principle upon which language family kinship is predicated. I have established that, even though 85% of the vocabulary of English has been adopted from Latin and French, based on the fact that the English language has retained its West Germanic grammar, the English language is classified as a West Germanic language.

I have established that the language of the descendants of enslaved Niger-Congo Africans in America has a Niger-Congo African grammar with English and other European words superimposed. I have established that the Pidgin/Creolists acknowledge that the language of the descendants of enslaved Niger-Congo Africans has a Niger-Congo African grammar with English and other European words superimposed. I have shown that even though the Pidgin/Creolists adhere to the principle of common origin and continuity in the rules of grammar as their criterion and basis for classifying English as a West Germanic language, where the language of the descendants of enslaved Africans in America is concerned, the Pidgin/Creolists abandon this criteria as their basis for positing language family kinship. I have shown that, predicated instead, on a criterion of the dominant lexifier or parent language from which the bulk of the vocabulary is derived, the Pidgin/Creolists posit the language spoken by the descendants of enslaved Africans in America as being a dialect of English, akin to the Germanic language family to which English belongs. I have shown that, just as the English language is not classified as a Romance language, based on the fact that the bulk of the English lexicon or vocabulary is derived from Latin and French, the language of the descendants of enslaved Africans cannot be classified as English merely because the bulk of the lexicon is, supposedly, derived from English.

I have shown that, predicated on the diachronic and comparative linguistic criteria of common origin and continuity of the rules of grammar, i.e., the scientific criterion for positing linguistic family kinship, there is no empirical evidence that an AAVE even exists. That is, the proponents of the AAVE thesis have not produced a single speech community in America or in the entire African diaspora where the descendants of enslaved Africans speak a hybrid African and English dialect or vernacular that has a Germanic (English) grammar with African words superimposed. In fact, as I have shown, predicated on the criteria of the dominant lexifier or parent language from which the bulk of the vocabulary is derived, the Pidgin/Creolist posit AAVE as being a dialect of English. However, the fact is, the bulk of the English lexicon is, itself, actually derived from the Romance languages. This fact constitutes an oxymoron that collapses the Pidgin/Creolists' dominant lexifier thesis on its own criteria.

Concerning the Pidgin-Creolists' postulation that the language of the descendants of enslaved Africans has undergone a de-creolization that has brought their AAVE dialect closer to the mainstream English dialect, and their claim that there has not been enough "divergence" from the mainstream English dialect to be considered a separate language, this is pure nonsense. The diachronic linguistic fact is that the language of enslaved Niger-Congo Africans emanates from a totally different linguistic continuum than the English language. Therefore, on the issue of how much linguistic 'divergence' from the Germanic English language has occurred, Negative! The issue is not how much linguistic 'divergence' from the Germanic English language has occurred. The issue is whether, as a result of the linguistic 'convergence' of the Niger-Congo African and Germanic English languages, the Niger-Congo African language of enslaved Africans has become genetically akin to the Germanic English language family. Corroboration of my contention regarding "linguistic divergence" versus "linguistic convergence" is found in William Welmers' book, *African Language Structures*. Describing the consequence of historical linguistic separation of two groups from the same linguistic continuum, Welmers (1973) states:

> Assume that a linguistically homogeneous community splits into two groups, through a process such as migration or invasion that creates a geographical separation between them. As long as neither group completely gives up its own language to adopt the language of some other people, there will now be two separate generation-to-generation continua. Linguistic changes will take place within each continuum, but many or all changes will be different for the two. After a few generations, members of the two groups, if reunited, will still be able to understand each other, though there will be peculiarities in each other's speech. But after several centuries, enough diverse changes will have accumulated so that members of the two groups will no longer be able to communicate with each other. They may then be said to speak different languages, each of which is equally a direct descendant of the original common language. (p. 3)

With regards to the type of linguistic change that occurs as a consequence of historical separation into two very different but still related linguistic groups, Welmers (1973) states:

> Some of the changes that have taken place in each are internal – that is, languages change even apart from contact with other languages. Some of the changes, on the other hand, may be, and usually are the result of external influences; the most conspicuous of such changes is the adoption of foreign words. But no matter how extensive the external influences have been, each resultant language has had a continuous history from its point of origin, the common parent language. Such languages are indeed genetically related, and for several millennia the relationship will remain apparent in parallels discoverable by well established techniques of comparative linguistics. The similarities of either language to other languages, created by such phenomena as borrowed vocabulary, do not constitute "relationship" or "affiliation;" they merely attest to contact. (pp. 3-4)

Thus, I maintain that Ebonics is not a dialect or vernacular of English, and any appellation that implies, inherently, by the use of the word English that Ebonics is related to the Germanic language family to which English belongs, is counterfeit.

REFERENCES

Alleyne, M. (1969). Linguistic Continuity of Africa in the Caribbean. In Richards, H. J. (Ed.), *Topics in Afro-American Studies*, pp. 118-128. New York: Black Academy Press.

Asante, M. K., & Asante K.W. (1991). *African Culture: The Rhythms of Unity*. Trenton: Africa World Press.

Asante M. K. (1998). *The Afrocentric Idea*. Philadelphia: Temple University Press.

Asante M. K. (1999). *The Painful Demise of Eurocentrism*. Trenton: Africa World Press, Inc.

Bailey, B. L. (1977). Jamaican Creole. In Hymes, D. (Ed.), *Pidginization and Creolization of Languages*, pp. 341-348. New York: Cambridge University Press.

Baugh J. (2000). *Beyond Ebonics: Linguistic Pride and Racial Prejudice*. New York: Oxford University Press.

Bennett, J. (1909).Gullah: A Negro Patois. *South Atlantic Quarterly*, October 1908 & January 1909.

Bickerton, D. (1975). *Dynamics of a Creole System*. New York: Cambridge University Press.

Blackshire-Belay, C.A. (1991). *Language and Literature in the African American Imagination*. Westport, CT: Greenwood Press.

Blackshire-Belay, C. A. (1996). The Location of Ebonics within the Framework of the Africological Paradigm. *Journal of Black Studies*, 27 (1): 5–23.

Blackshire-Belay, C. A. The Linguistic Dimensions of Global Africa: Ebonics as International Languages of African Peoples. In Crawford, C. (Ed.), *Ebonics and Language Education*. New York: Sankofa World Publishers.

Callewart, D. M., & Genyea, J. (1980). *Basic Chemistry General, Organic, Biological.* New York: Worth Publishers.

Chambers, J. Jr. (Ed.). (1983). *Black English: Educational Equity and the Law.* Ann Arbor: Karoma.

Crystal D. (1997). *A Dictionary of Linguistics and Phonetics.* Malden Blackwell Publishers.

Curtin, P. D. (1976). Measuring the Atlantic Slave Trade Once Again. *Journal of African History, 17.*

DeCamp, D. (1977). Introduction: The Study of Pidgin and Creole Languages. In Hymes, D. (Ed.), *Pidginization and Creolization of Languages*, pp. 13-39. New York: Cambridge University Press.

Dillard, J. L. (1972). *Black English Its History and Usage in the United States.* New York: Random House.

Dillard, J. L. (1976). *American Talk.* New York: Vintage Books.

Duncan, G. (2003). Talkin' That Talk: Language, Culture, and Education in African America. In Smitherman, G. (Ed.), *International Journal of Qualitative Studies in Education*, 16(5): 737-739.

Duncan, G., & Jackson, R. (2004). The Language We Cry In: Black Language Practice at a Post-Desegregated Urban High School. *GSE Perspectives on Urban Education*, 3(1).Retrieved from http://www.urbanedjournal.org/articles/article0014.html.

_____ (2004). Ebonics and Education: A Critical Appraisal of the Post-1996 Research Literature. *African American Research Perspectives*, Spring/Summer, 188-198.

_____ (2006). Discourse, Cultural Imperialism, and Black Culture and Language Research in the United States. In Shi-xu (Ed.), *Discourses as Cultural Struggle*, pp. 155-168. Hong Kong: Hong Kong University Press.

Elkins, S. (1971). *Slavery*, (2nd ed.). Chicago: University of Chicago Press.

Franklin, J. H. (1980). *From Slavery to Freedom: A History of Negro Americans*. New York: Alfred Knopf.

Fromkin, V. & Rodman, R. (1978). *An Introduction to Language* (2nd ed.). New York: Holt Rinehart and Winston.

_____ (1993). (5th ed.).

Gonzales, A. E. (1922). *The Black Border; Gullah, Stories of the Carolina Coast*. Columbia, S.C.

Greenberg, J. H. (1967). *Essays in Linguistics*. Chicago: University of Chicago Press.

Hall, R. A., Jr. (1962). The Life Cycle of Languages. In *Lingua* 11:152-6.

Hartmann, R. R. K. & Stork, F. C. (1976). *Dictionary of Language and Linguistics*. New York: John Wiley &Sons.

Herron, J. D. (1981). *Understanding Chemistry: A Preparatory Course.* New York: Random House

Hymes D. (1977). (Ed.). *Pidginization and Creolization of Languages*. London/New York: Cambridge University Press.

Jahn, J. (1961). *Muntu: An Outline of the New African Culture*. New York: Grove Press.

Johnson, G. B. (1930). *Folk Culture on St. Helena Island, South Carolina.* Chapel Hill: University of North Carolina Press.

Joiner, C. Judge. (1979).*Memorandum Opinion and Order,* United States District Court. *Martin Luther King Junior Elementary School Children, et al. vs. Ann Arbor School District Board.* Detroit.

Key, M. R. (1973). *The History of Black English.* Paper Presented at Cognitive and Language Development in the Black Child Conference. St. Louis, MO.

Kamarah, S. *Re: Creole or Krio.* Internet e-mail number skamarah@ emmanuel.

Kotz, J. C. & Purnell, K. F. (1987). *Chemistry & Chemical Reactivity.* Philadelphia: Saunders College Publishing

Krapp, G. P. (1924). *The English of the Negro.* New York: American Mercury.

Lehmann, W. P. (1973). *Historical Linguistics: An Introduction.* New York: Holt Rhinehart & Winston.

Lynd, S. (1967). *Class Conflict, Slavery, and the United States Constitution: Ten Essays.* Indianapolis: Bobbs-Merrill.

Palmer, L. R. (1978). *Descriptive and Comparative Linguistics: A Critical Introduction.* London: Faber &Faber.

Payen-Bellisle, R. (1894). *Sons et Formes du Creole dans les Antilles.* Baltimore: Murphy.

Perry T., & Delpit, L. (1997).Oakland School Board Resolution No. 9697 0063, December 18, 1996. In *Real Ebonics Debate.* Boston: Beacon Press.

Rickford, J. R. (1997). Suite for Ebony and Phonics, *Discover, 18(12),* 82.

Romaine, S. (1994). *Language and Society: An Introduction to Sociolinguistics.* New York: Oxford University Press, Inc.

Schuchardt, H. (1909). *Die Lingua franca In Zeitschrift fur romanische Philologie* 33: 441-461.

Smith, E. A. (1976). A Case for Bilingual and Bicultural Education for United States Slave Descendants of African Origin. Seminar Paper, Series #39. California State University-Fullerton.

Smitherman, G. (1977). *Talkin and Testifying: The Language of Black America*. Boston: Houghton Mifflin.

Smitherman,G. (1997). Black English/Ebonics: What It Be Like? Milwaukee. *Rethinking Schools, Fall,12(1), 8*.

Stewart, William A. (1962). *Creole Languages in the Caribbean Study of the Role of Second Languages in Asia, Africa, and Latin America.* In Rice, F. A. (Ed.).,Washington D.C.: Center for Applied Linguistics, 34-53.

_____(1973). Toward a History of American Negro Dialect. In Williams, F. (Ed.) *Language and Poverty,* (pp. 372-379). Chicago: Rand McNally College Publishing Company.

Turner, L. D. (1965). *Krio Texts with Grammatical Notes and Translations in English*. Chicago: Roosevelt University.

Turner, L. D. (1973). *Africanisms in the Gullah Dialect*. Ann Arbor: University of Michigan Press.

Twiggs, R. (1973). *Pan African Language in the Western Hemisphere*. Quincy, MA: Christopher.

Vass, W. K. (1979). *The Bantu Speaking Heritage of the United States*. Los Angeles: University of California.

Webster's Collegiate Dictionary (10th ed.),(2001), 1308.

Welmers, W. E. (1973). *African Language Structures*. Berkeley: University of California Press.

Whinnom, K. (1977). Linguistic Hybridization and the Special Case of Pidgins and Creoles. In Hymes,D. (Ed.), *Pidginizaton and Creolization of Languages* (pp. 91-115). New York: Cambridge

University Press. [See also Whinnom, K. (1956). The Origin of the European Based Creoles and Pidgins. *Orbis,*509.]

Williams, R., (Ed.). 1975. *Ebonics: The True Language of Black Folks*. St. Louis: Institute of Black Studies.

Williams, R. (1997, January 28).Ebonics as a Bridge to Standard English, *St. Louis Post-Dispatch*: 14.

Williams, R. (Ed.) 1997. The Ebonics controversy. *The Journal of Black Psychology*: 208.

Wofford, J. (1979). Ebonics: A Legitimate System of Oral Communication, *Journal of Black Studies*: 367-381.

Woodson, C. G. (1933). The *Miseducation of the Negro*. Washington, DC: The Associated Publishers.

2

EBONICS: RE-CLAIMING AND RE-DEFINING OUR LANGUAGE

Robert L. Williams, Ph.D.

Dr. Williams inspired everyone at the 7th annual Ebonics Conference (2004) with this message. Held in Los Angeles, California, this conference stressed the importance of there being effective communication in medical environments between medical and healthcare providers and their African American patients.

Originally, I come from Little Rock, Arkansas. It is a long ways from Little Rock to Los Angeles. However, for your information Little Rock and Arkansas are the only City and State whose names are cited in the King James Holy Bible. "And David killed Goliath with a 'Little Rock', and "Noah looked out of the 'Ark and Saw' that the waters were gone".

One of the reasons that I became involved with the, so-called, Black language controversy and the IQ test controversy is that I was virtually one of the causalities. I had grown sick and tired of hearing about the intellectual deficiencies of Black children and their linguistic deficits. When I was in the tenth grade at Dunbar High School in Little Rock, Arkansas, I was given an IQ test. I spoke Ebonics frequently and fluently. I tested out in the slow group because I earned an IQ score of 82. My counselor told me that I barely missed the <u>Mentally Retarded</u> classes by 3 IQ points. But when she told me my score, I smiled thinking that an 82 was at least a grade of B or B minus. Instead, she told me that I was not college material and, consequently, enrolled me in a vocational trade curriculum. As a consequence, in High school, I took auto mechanics, bricklaying, electricity and carpentry—the usual vocational trade courses. I did slip into some English, math and science courses.

Through a fluke I managed to go to Philander Smith College, a Historically Black College in Little Rock. I graduated in the class with Minnie Joyce Jones, a.k.a. Dr. Jocelyn Elders, with honors and ranked in the top five, won distinction in my field, and graduated CUM LAUDE, LAWDY LAWDY, AND THANK YOU LAWDY. From there, I left DOWN SOUTH and went to Wayne State University in Detroit (UP SOUTH) because in those days (1953) Blacks were not allowed to enroll in all-white graduate programs in the South.

Today we are celebrating the 1954 Brown V. Topeka decision. On May 17, 1954, I was a graduate student at Wayne State University. I did not realize the impact of the Brown decision at that time. I have been invited to speak at the annual Brown symposium on several occasions. From Wayne State I went on to Washington University to gain a doctorate in Clinical Psychology in 1961, 43 years ago, the first African American to do so in Psychology at Washington University-St. Louis. Let me state my position on the matters of Black IQ and language deficiency at the outset:

1) Black Americans are not intellectually, emotionally, spiritually, or psychologically inferior to any other race of people—white, brown, red or yellow Americans.

2) The real and central issue is not whether Black Americans are less intelligent than other Americans, but rather the issues are the over-representation in special education classes, the serious under educational achievement, mis-education, and the dis-education of our African American children. Current achievement test data indicate that no urban school district is effectively educating the African American student, and the dropout rate has reached crisis proportions.

3) African Americans do not speak an inferior language. We may speak a different language, but a difference is not necessarily a deficiency.

Dr. Bill Cosby stirred up a big controversy in some blistering words against lower social economic families. Cosby is criticized by some and supported by other Blacks for remarks he made in Washington, D.C. at the NAACP celebration of <u>Brown v. Board of Education</u>. To the *Washington Post*, Cosby ridiculed "lower economic people". Here are a couple of Cosby's zingers that shocked the crowd:

> Lower [African American] economic people are not holding up their end in this deal. These people are not parenting. They are buying things for kids --$500 sneakers for what? And won't spend $200 for 'Hooked on Phonics'.

His blistering words continued:

> They're standing on the corner and they can't speak English. I can't even talk the way these people talk: "Why you aint." "Where you is."... and I blamed the kid until I heard the mother talk. And then I heard the father talk... Everybody knows it's important to speak English except these knuckleheads... You can't be a doctor with that kind of crap coming out of your mouth! (Wilson, p. a8, 2004)

Were Cosby's comments off target? Or did he give a rare Black voice to a hard issue for Blacks? The important point here is that these issues are not just academic issues; they are political, social, economic, psychological, educational, ethical and legal issues as well. "My language is me"; it is an extension and essence of my being, my existence. It is a reflection and badge of my culture and my family. Criticism of my language is, essentially, a direct attack on my self-esteem and cultural identity. It is very similar to criticizing my hair, my size or my physical make-up. Many African American children do not speak the, so-called, mainstream English during their early years of school. They speak a "home language" or EBONICS that is vastly different from the, so-called, mainstream English.

That language is the language they have heard and learned from their grandmas, grandpas, mamas and daddies, many of whom had very little formal education. By the time they enter elementary school, these children have internalized the basic features of the "home language". They do not know that they are not supposed to talk like that. They may even be penalized, teased and scolded for speaking Ebonics, and this criticism may continue through their elementary and secondary years. We have had integrated education for only 50 years. For many of us, if we look back three generations, our great grandparents were in slavery and had zero formal education. Racism may not be the only source of all the ills that beset the African American underclass, but it is a major factor.

In January 1973 I had grown sick and tired of being defined by white folks. I called a national conference of Black and White scholars to discuss the Cognitive and Language Development of African American Children. A significant incident occurred at that conference. The Black conferees were critical of the work done by white researchers on the language of Black folks. The Black conferees decided to caucus among themselves and define Black language from a Black perspective. It was during that caucus that I experienced an *epiphany*, a defining moment, or a sudden creative and intuitive insight. I coined the term *Ebonics* by combining two words: Ebony (Black) and phonics (speech sounds) to produce Ebonics. The coining of the term Ebonics was accomplished in the spirit of the *second Nguzo Saba Principle Kugichagulia* (self-determination), as defined by Maulana Karenga (1965).

The following is a partial re-creation of the spirited discussion that occurred concerning re-defining black language from a Black perspective:

Dr. Robert Williams: Ladies and gentlemen, we need to define what we speak. We need to give a clear definition of our language.

Dr. Ernie Smith: Let me tell you something. If you notice every language in the world represents a nation or a nationality. What we are speaking has continuity not only in the United States, but also outside of the United States and all the way back to the mother country. We need to get the term completely off the English (side of the) scale and start calling it what it really represents.

Dr. Williams: Let me make a point here. Language is a process of communication. But we need to deal with the root of our language. What about Ebo? Ebo-linguistics? Ebo-lingual? Ebo-phonics? Ebonics? *Let's define our language as Ebonics.*

The Group: That sounds real good.

Dr. Williams: I am talking about an Ebony language. We know that Ebony means Black and Phonics refers to speech sounds or the science of speech sounds. Thus, we are really talking about the science of Black speech sounds or language.

Dr. Ann Covington: That's beautiful.

Dr. Williams: With Ebonics we mean Black pronunciation, vocabulary, syntax, structure and the whole ball of wax.

Dr. Grace Holt: That's beautiful. Now we can go to a new term and really define it and say what our language really is.

Dr. Ernie Smith: Ebonics may be defined as the linguistic and paralinguistic features, which on a concentric continuum, represent the communicative competence of the West African, Caribbean, and United States slave descendants of African origin. It includes the grammar, various idioms, patois, argots, idiolects, and social dialects of Black people. Ebonics, also, includes nonverbal sounds, cues and gestures that are systematically and predictably utilized in the process of communication by African-Americans.

Kimani K. S. Nehusi (2001, pp. 62, 83), in an article "From Medew Netjer to Ebonics", connects the term "hbny" and "Ebony" to African origins: "hbny refers to a special kind of tree that predominated in Nubia, and was noted for its hard, black and beautiful wood.... hbny = Black, Beautiful and Durable".

Previous to the above conference, White linguists (Stewart, 1969; Dillard, 1972; Fasold, 1972) defined and described the language of African Americans. Their definitions of our language were pejorative descriptions: "Black English", "substandard speech", "deviant speech", "deficient speech", "non-standard English" and other negative terms. According to Aisha Blackshire-Belay (2001):

To these [white] individuals Ebonics is "nonsense," "made-up", and unscientific only because they did not create it themselves. However, the terms "Black English," "Black Vernacular English," "African American Vernacular English", were coined by [white] linguists, thus these terms are appropriate. (p. 166)

The Encarta World English Dictionary (1999, p. 565), not surprisingly, provides a rather limited definition of Ebonics, but an extensive definitive discussion of AAVE (African American Vernacular English). *The Encarta* defines AAVE as "the term used by scholars for the widespread and varied African American usages also called Ebonics, Afro-American English, American Black English, Black English, Black English Vernacular and Black Vernacular English."

I conducted a study to assess the so-called awareness of the terms AAVE, Black English and Ebonics. Not surprisingly, only 5 percent of the sample had heard of AAVE, about 50 percent Black English and 100 percent had heard of the term Ebonics. Thus, Ebonics clearly represented a response to the need for the proper naming (Nommo) and defining of our language. As Toni Morrison (1987:190) aptly puts it in her novel, *Beloved*: "Definitions belonged to the definers... not to the defined." Blackshire-Belay states (2001): "We know how significant the naming process is; therefore, we must act and become namers of our own actions and experiences, and not to be named by others" (p. 171).

We needed to define our language, not let others define it for us. The creation of new Black terminology and definitions, as in the case of Ebonics, however, was not a precedent. Other Black scholars had previously coined relevant terms and continue to do so. Dr. Maulana Karenga (1965, 1976 and 1980) introduced the terms *"Kwanzaa"* and *"Nguzo Saba"*, principles both of which have gained significant acceptance among African Americans.

Dr. Molefi Asante introduced *Afrocentricity*. He states (1998, p. 2), "The crystallization of this critical perspective I have named *Afrocentricity*, which means, literally, placing African ideals at the center of any analysis that involves African culture and behavior". Dr. Bobby Wright (1976) coined *Mentacide* which means "...the deliberate and systematic destruction of an individual or group's mind" by distorting and omitting the group's history. Dr. Clenora Hudson-Weems (1993) is credited with coinage of the term *Africana Womanism*. She states (1993):

Africana Womanism is a term I coined and defined in 1987...[It] is an ideology created and designed for all women of African descent. It is grounded in African culture, and... therefore, it necessarily focuses on the unique experiences, struggles, needs, and desires of Africana women. (pp. 20-21)

Further, prior to December 18, 1996, not too many people had heard of the term Ebonics. On that date the Oakland California School Board passed a resolution legitimizing Ebonics as a language to be used as a bridge to teach the English language. The School Board's decision created a firestorm of controversy. Following the resolution, there was, however, a disturbing rush to judgment on the merits of Ebonics. The media's negative spin on Ebonics created many misconceptions about the term.

The central issue in the School Board's decision was not whether Ebonics qualified as a legitimate language, but whether Black children were getting the education they deserved. The evidence suggested they were not. The school system faced a crisis. Fifty-three percent of the students in the Oakland School District were Black. Their mean grade point average was 1.8 (D plus), and a disproportionate number of students in special education classes were Black (71%). Sixty-four percent of the students retained were African American. Eighty percent of all suspended students were African American. In addition, almost twenty percent of the Black students who reached the 12th grade did not graduate. Combining these statistics with the fact that sixty-one percent of the teachers in the Oakland School District were white, one can easily see that the District faced a crisis, which the Board attempted to resolve.

If Ebonics is not a language, then tell me what is it? Is it a dialect? Is it slang? Is it deficient speech? Is it speech of the uneducated? There are two schools of thought on the origin of Ebonics: (a) the Pidgin/Creole theory and (b) the African Retention theory. First, the Pidgin/Creole theory states that on the plantation, a common language, by necessity, emerged among the captives or the prisoners. A simplified version of the English language emerged that was defined as or called the pidgin language. This language served as the lingua franca, or the language used for communication between persons of different mother tongues. Pidgin is not the native language for any of the speakers. Pidgin has no native speakers. Pidgin language is reduced in vocabulary. One theory is that pidgin language developed from the Portuguese language. Others have been unwilling to accept this version of Black language and say that these pidgins are not merely distortions of European languages, but bear some resemblance to West African languages. The Creole has pidgin as its source. It is the language that the children of the captives learned as their first language.

Another point that I make is that, when you superimpose a second language on the native tongue, an interesting combination or interference occurs, and this depends on the basic structure of the native language. For example, the Cantonese dialect of Chinese has no [r] in the syllable initial position of their dialect. So they pronounce [r] as [l]. Hence, "Fried Rice" as "Flied Lice" and Robert Redford as Lobut Ledfud. [See Fromkin and Rodman, (1993, p.197)]. Blackshire-Belay adds (2001):

> This "getting in the way," called "interference" refers to the tendency of individuals to make the language they are learning conform to the sound and structure of their native tongues. For example Polish immigrants attempting to speak English made English sound like Polish and German immigrants made English sound like German. (p. 174)

The second school of thought is that of the Africologist/Africanist or African Retention School. The proponents of this view contend that Africans, in spite of Whites attempting to strip away their culture, retained much of their cultural and linguistic identity. Because they were isolated and segregated on the plantation, with adaptations due to the conditions of enslavement, they retained their religion, philosophy, culture, folkways, beliefs, tales and storytelling, naming practices, art, kinship and music. How can we not be aware of the transmission of such a rich African oral tradition that kindles our communicative behavior?

From the outset, the art of storytelling, song, praise-singing, myth-making and poetry was retained. The Brer Rabbit folktales, lullabies of Black mothers, work and blues songs of enslaved women and men laborers, street cries of vendors, spirituals, call and response sermons of Black preachers, fables, rhymes, proverbs and healing chants—all are clear African retentions.

Africanisms represent the deep structure of Ebonics. Many West African languages such as Ibo, Twi, Fon, Yoruba, Wolof, Fante, Mandinka, and others are relatives of Ebonics or Black Language. Dr. Ernie Smith (1977) contends:

> Ebonics is the African American's linguistic memory of Africa applied to English words. It is the linguistic continuation of Africa in Black America. To dismiss or negate Ebonics as a legitimate language of African–descended people is to negate our universal memory of Africa.

Many whites would have us believe that the enslaved Africans arrived on this continent empty handed; no culture, dumb and ignorant. That is not the case. To the contrary, Baraka states (1963):

> It is absurd to assume, as has been the tendency, among a great many Western anthropologists and sociologists, that all traces of Africa were erased from the Negro's mind because he learned English. The very nature of the English the Negro spoke and still speaks drops the lie on that idea. (p.9)

Holloway reported on the Bantus as an example of African Retention. He states (1996):

Once the Bantu reached America they were able to retain much of their cultural identity. Enforced isolation of these Africans by plantation owners allowed them to retain their religion, philosophy, culture, folklore, folkways, folk beliefs, folk tales, storytelling, naming practices, home economics, arts, kinship and music. The Africanisms were shared and adopted by the various African ethnic groups of the field slave community, and they gradually developed into African American cooking (soul food), music (jazz, blues, spirituals, gospels), language, religion, philosophy, customs and arts. (p. 17)

Charges have been made that Ebonics has no utility within the lives of African Americans. My research refutes this negative assertion. Several studies have suggested how the use of Ebonics raised standardized test and reading scores of African American children. The first study by Williams and Rivers (1975, p. 104) translated (code switched) test items contained in a standardized test of Basic Concepts from Standard English to Ebonics, or into a language that was familiar to the children. The results were striking. The children who scored low on the Standard English version performed exceptionally well on the Ebonics version. The following are two examples of how we changed the test items:

> Standard English: Mark the toy that is <u>behind</u> the sofa.
> Ebonics: Mark the toy that is <u>in back of </u>the couch.
> Standard English: Point to the squirrel that <u>is beginning</u> to climb the tree.
> Ebonics: Point to the squirrel that is <u>fixing to climb</u> the tree.

In another study involving the Peabody Picture Vocabulary Test, Dr. Wendell Rivers (1977) translated (code switched) items from the standard version to an Ebonics version. Instead of asking the child to identify a "crib" as the test item required, the child was asked to identify a baby bed. Crib to many African children meant a house or an apartment. With the code switching, the children's IQs increased significantly.

What was discovered was that the standard versions contained Blocking agents or noise. In many ways the Standard English version did not activate the Black children's linguistic conceptual systems. Rather, the blocking agents or noise interfered with the children's understanding of the question. This does not mean that Black children lacked the capacity to process standard language. Instead, the children's linguistic intake gates were not activated by the stimulus properties of Standard English. Many African American children must be taught to translate (code switch) - to move from Ebonics to Standard English, just as Asian or Hispanic children must be taught to move from their native tongues to Standard English.

Dr. Savannah Young (1997) provides an excellent guide for teaching Standard English to Ebonics speaking children. She provides exercises for parents and teachers, and demonstrates how to help children learn Standard English.

In his powerful book, *The Throwaway Kids*, Dr. Gary Simpkins explains the research on an Ebonics oriented reading program. Developed by Simpkins, Holt and Simpkins (1974) the BRIDGE READING PROGRAM places emphasis on using language skills already in the child's repertoire. Bridge is a transitional process by which students process from the familiar (Ebonics) to the less familiar (Standard American English - SAE). It embraces the axiom "Start where the child is". The Bridge program uses three readers to present the same story. The first story is written 100% in Ebonics, the second 50% in Ebonics and 50% in SAE and the third 100% in SAE.

Two groups (a Bridge-trained group and a non-Bridge trained group) were each given different reading programs over a 4-month period. At the end of the training period, they were given the Iowa Test of Basic Skills. The Bridge group showed a 6.2 - month increase in their reading scores, whereas the non-Bridge group reading scores increased only 1.6 months. These findings were significant. Clearly, these three studies demonstrate the effectiveness of recognizing and using the home language (in this case Ebonics) as a bridge to teach SAE.

There is considerable confusion surrounding the education of African American Children. We have been led to believe certain fallacies concerning the education of Black and other minority children. Further, the rising number of high school dropouts is one of the most dramatic indicators suggesting that school systems may have dual purposes for educating Black children. Does the American educational system have a dual purpose for Black children?

What is the purpose of American education? Is it to properly educate children, or is it to prepare them to take their place in American society? On the one hand, the educational system is failing to educate our African American children, who are disproportionately represented in Special Education classes. One in every four Black students enrolled in the ninth grade drops out before high school graduation. Dropout rates for Black students are just under twice as great as for white children.

On the other hand, the educational system has not failed Black children, especially if the purpose is to prepare them to take their place in society. Schools are doing what they are supposed to do. They are organizing Black children for the purpose of taking their place in society. And they are succeeding at what they are designed to do. Thus, the school systems really have not failed. They are doing a good job at preparing Black children to take their place in society—at the bottom of the rung of the economic ladder and in prisons (slave ships that don't float). Perhaps, it is not explicitly stated as a policy, but that is what is happening; it is de facto, existing in fact but without a policy.

A recent study suggests that Black and Hispanic elementary school children enjoy school more and have greater confidence in their own academic abilities than their white classmates. Three researchers at the University of Michigan's Center wrote this study for Human Growth and Development. It challenges the popular belief that minority children's poor academic achievement is a function of low self-esteem, a lack of educational motivation and low academic ability. More significantly are questions the study raises about what goes wrong for these children later on in junior high and high school. At that point, their academic performance and attitudes toward school often deteriorate markedly. Blacks and Hispanics show the largest percentages of dropouts and failure to complete high school.

Kunjufu (1986) argues that despair sets in much earlier than Junior High school. He posits a Fourth Grade Syndrome in which Black males, in particular, become disillusioned with school. This is a period when they begin, psychologically, to drop out or fall out of school. Previously bright eager young boys begin to hate school.

If our Black men and women and our Black boys and girls can become super athletes and Olympic gold medalists, they also can become super businessmen and women, doctors, professors, lawyers, accountants, and rocket scientists at all the high level positions. We must demand that the educational systems develop Black scholars and Black scholar athletes and not just Black athletes–a.k.a.ones with a Jock Strap Mentality. We must require more scholastic trophies, in addition to the numerous athletic trophies in the halls of elementary schools and high schools.

The question concerning the education or mis-education of Blacks is explicated in a metaphor used by Professor Lani Guinier of Harvard University Law School in her book *The Miner's Canary*. She points out that years ago, coal miners used a canary to detect dangerous levels of methane gas present in the mines. The bird, having a more delicate respiratory system than the miners, would succumb to the gas long before the miners detected it, thereby warning the miners of the dangers of toxic substances in the mines. In a similar fashion, Blacks are the canaries. They are more sensitive to and affected by the deficiencies in the educational system than are Whites because, as victims, they have a keener awareness of its lethal effects.

The overrepresentation of Blacks in Special Education programs and the high dropout rates are grim warnings to the general population that the educational system is toxic to many Black children. Just as the canary warned the miners of toxicity in the mines, these warnings from the African American Children must be heeded. Instead, the problem is being located in the canary or in the African American children, who are the victims, rather than in the environment or in the educational system. Professor Guinier warns how we pathologize the canary and act as though the solution is to fix the canary, to fit it with a tiny gas mask so that it can withstand the toxic atmosphere. She maintains that we must cease arguing about what is wrong with the canary, seek to remedy the conditions under which it exists, and make changes in those circumstances.

We must use the overrepresentation in special education classes to fix the educational system in order to eliminate the toxic effects on the Black children. Professor Guinier says that perhaps Black kids are America's canaries; their failure and their social dysfunction warns us of the toxins in the classrooms. The question is what do we do about what these Black canaries are telling us? Instead of trying to find out what is wrong with the canary or compiling statistics on the canary, we need to pay more attention to the atmospheric toxicity. The canaries have told us enough.

Now that we have entered the 21st century, this nation cannot afford to leave underdeveloped the talents of millions of children who happen to be born different by virtue of race, language, sex, income status or mental ability. Nor can this nation ignore, under the pretense of educational excellence, the unfinished national task of offering every child—Black, Hispanic, Native American, Asian and White—an equal chance to learn and to become a self-sufficient and productive citizen. President Bush's policy of "No Child Left Behind" is a clear mandate to educators.

It is my firm belief that education is a fundamental right deserving protection under the 14th amendment, which guarantees all Americans equal protection of the law. Democracy does not guarantee success, but it is supposed to guarantee equal opportunity. I further believe that progress for African Americans will accelerate when we are able to build on the knowledge provided by our ancestors, and pass it on to the succeeding generations. When we forget this knowledge, or when we omit this information in our educational process, or when this knowledge is distorted, whether by accident or design, a terrible condition is created.

Thus, as we survey the historical and current state of affairs of African Americans, we notice a familiar litany of rather negative and pathological descriptions or euphemisms of African Americans. For example, for Blacks we associate words and phrases like slavery, underprivileged, gangs, drugs, crime, unemployment, teenage pregnancy, school failure, school dropout, welfare and, seemingly, an endless litany of euphemisms suggesting deficits and weaknesses of African Americans. I believe that when we write and infuse our educational system, Afrocentrically, with an African-centered perspective as advanced by Molefi Asante (1987), we will have a different group of African American children who will be eager and willing to learn.

I am suggesting a bold, new educational paradigm for our African American Students. Afrocentric education is a systematic and comprehensive method of equipping our children with the proper education to effectively deal with life's problems and to meet the challenges that confront them. Afrocentric education represents a paradigm shift. And that is what we need in public schools, because too many educational systems have developed what Barker (1986) called a "paradigm paralysis" which means getting stuck on a particular method, playing it safe and refusing to look at alternative methods of teaching.

Barker (1986) provides a classic example of paradigm paralysis involving Swiss watchmakers, who in 1960 commanded approximately 65% of the world market in watch making. When one of their watchmakers invented the Quartz watch, the Swiss Corporate Executives rejected the new paradigm, because, to them, a watch without a mainspring was not a watch. Because it did not have any movable parts, it did not fit their "watch paradigm". Since the Swiss Executives rejected the new paradigm and did not protect the Quartz patent, Seiko and Texas Instruments pre-empted their discovery and became world leaders in watch making. Swiss lost their watch preeminence in watch-making because they refused to change their paradigm. They were guilty of paradigm paralysis.

I firmly believe that progress will evolve from the Ebonics controversy and debate. I also believe that the debate gave our nation an opportunity to engage in thoughtful discussion and dialogue that could lead to new policies and practices in teacher education programs. The real issue remains: the academic underachievement of our African American children. It is clearly in the nation's best interest to produce African American children who can speak, read, write and comprehend Standard American English, and at the same time, preserve the rich cultural heritage of our people. Ebonics offers a means by which the end goal can be realized.

REFERENCES

Asante, M. K. (1987). *The Afrocentric Idea*. Philadelphia: Temple University Press.

Barker, J. (1986). "Discovering the Future: The Business of Paradigms," (videotape).

Dillard, J.L. (1972). *Black English: Its History and Usage in the United States*. New York: Random House.

Encarta World English Dictionary (1999). New York: St. Martin's Press.

Fasold, R.W. (1972). *Tense Marking in Black English*. Washington D.C.: Center for Applied Linguistics.

Fromkin, V. & Rodman R. (1993). *An Introduction to Language*. New York: Harcourt Brace.

Hill, P.L. (Ed.). (1997). *Call and Response: The Riverside Anthology of the African American Literary Tradition*, Boston: Houghton-Mifflin.

Holloway, J. E. (1996). "The Origins of African American Culture." In J.E. Holloway (Ed.) *Africanisms in American Culture*, Bloomington: Indiana University Press.

Hudson-Weems, C. (1993). *Africana Womanism: Reclaiming Ourselves*. Troy, Michigan: Bedford Publishers, Inc.

Karenga, M. (1976). *Kwanzaa: Origin, Concepts, Practice*. Los Angeles: Kawaida Publications.

Karenga, M. (1965). *Nguzo Saba*. San Diego: Kawaida Publications.

Kunjufu, J. (1986). *Countering the Conspiracy to Destroy Black Boys*, Volume II, Chicago: African American Images.

Morrison, T. (1987). *Beloved*. New York: Alfred A. Knopf.

Outlaw, L. (1987). *Africology: Normative Theory. Symposium on Africology*. Department of African American Studies, University of Wisconsin, Milwaukee.

Rivers, L.W. (1977). *Black Language: A Moderator Variable in Intelligence*. National Institute of Mental Health Grant #5R 01 MH 24454-03.

Simpkins, G., Holt, G., & Simpkins. (1974). *Bridge: A Cross-Culture Reading Program. Experimental Edition*. Boston: Houghton-Mifflin.

Smith, E. (1997). *Ebonics: A Threat to White Supremacy*. A Presentation at the United African Movement, (U.A.M.) Forum, New York, (videotape).

Stewart, W., Baratz, J.C. & Shuy, R. (Eds.) (1969). *On the Use of Negro Dialect in Teaching of Reading*, Washington, D.C.: Center for Applied Linguistics.

Williams, R.L. & Rivers, L.W. (1975). The Effects of Language on the Test Performance of Black Children. In R.L. Williams (Ed.), Ebonics: *The True Language of Black Folks*. St. Louis: The Institute of Black Studies.

Williams, R.L. (2002). *A Language Survey of African American Vernacular English, Black English and Ebonics*, Unpublished Manuscript.

Wright, B. (1976). *Mentacide: The Ultimate Threat to the Black Race*. Unpublished Manuscript.

Young, S. (1997). *A Guide to American English*, St. Louis: Miller-Young.

3

EBONICS IS MOST RELEVANT

It is axiomatic that the best medium for teaching a child is his mother tongue. Psychologically, it is the system of meaningful signs that in his mind works automatically for expression and understanding. Sociologically, it is a means of identification among the members of the community to which he belongs. Educationally, he learns more quickly through it than through an unfamiliar linguistic medium. (UNESCO, 1953, p.11)

Twenty-four years ago, I undertook to produce a light-hearted book of the words and the phrases that Black folks in America use that others do not use. I had no idea that I was being *called* into the study of Ebonics, the "true language of Black folks" (Williams, 1975). I learned, early-on, however, that this was a serious endeavor—not an undertaking that was to be taken lightly. I was *chosen* to become an Africologist, to study the truth about Ebonics from an African "agency or centeredness" (Blackshire-Belay, 1996, p. 6), and then further that truth. Later, after being shown the vision of what equal educational opportunities for Ebonics-speaking, Black children and youths would mean, i.e., better psychological, educational, social and, in the long run, better economic development/empowerment, I 'could not turn back my hand from the plough'. I had been chosen "to root out, and to pull down, and to destroy and to throw down, to build, and to plant" for the good of Ebonics-speakers.

By now, it is known that, in this Book, Ebonics is not being used as a synonym for "Black English (BE), African-American English (AAE), African-American Vernacular English (AAVE), or as any term that incorporates the term "English" in it when describing or denoting the speech and language of Blacks in America. As in the case of the ultimate meaning of the created phrase, "Black Lives Matter", Ebonics, as a subject and a force, has extreme relevance that is being denied equal rights as a language: It is being mislabeled. It is being struck down when its relevance is on the verge of being acknowledged and reckoned with. It is being shortchanged into merely being a dialect of English. At the mention of its name, people show reactions of hostility and hatred. The attempt has been made to annihilate it from its existence by erroneous reports of its creation and its composition. Therefore, speakers of Ebonics continue to fail in all aspects of education, employment and social standing. So, on a lesser plane, 'Ebonics matters' is in direct relationship to the fact that "Black lives matter", and if any phrase should be allowed to ride the tide of the significance of the word "matter", it should be 'Ebonics matters'. However, in homage to the purity and seriousness of the concept that "Black lives matter", Chapter 3 will not be entitled "Ebonics Matters", but, simply, though, profoundly, "Ebonics Is Most Relevant".

This book, *Introduction to Ebonics*, was conceived to be written as a Work that would portray how most Black people in America, particularly in the South, sound differently from Caucasians who speak English, even when they use the same words (Scott, 1998, p. 191-195) (See Chapter 5 of this Work.). Most Blacks, also, use a host of sentence structures that are different from English-speaking Caucasians (Simpkins, 2002) and, many times, Blacks have created different meanings for familiar English words that Caucasians use (This phenomenon will be fully examined in the pending publication: *Introduction to Ebonics, Volume II* of this Work.). All that was or is needed is to listen to a two-year-old child from ninety percent of the Black households in this country (Blackshire-Belay in Crawford, 2001, p.174). Out of the mouth of that babe will come what he has heard all of his language learning life: Ebonics -- like it or not.

"Mahmee, daat monkee gohn giht mee"? [Mommy, is that monkey going to get me?] (Personal communication, Josiah Redmond Taylor, 1998, when he was two years old)

It is true that bold steps were taken in 1973 by the Africologists who defined Ebonics as being an African language, and I will stand boldly upon that foundation. This is for sure; a Black person cannot hide what is going on in his family's language base or roots. The attempt to disguise the truth that English is not his mother tongue, with sprinklings of, so-called, "good" English, many times results in ungrammatical utterances that reveal very deep structure retentions of Niger-Congo African Ebonics -- For Ebonics is what is in his mind and soul, and when least expected, the nuances of Ebonics *gohn* slip out.

"Hope en Paul hih-uh, Mahmee?"[Are Hope and Paul here, Mommy?] (Personal communication, Josiah Redmond Taylor, 1998, when he was two years old)

Since most Ebonics-speaking Africans in the Diaspora still live in social isolation from Caucasians more hours than they are with them, the speech and language patterns that their forefathers retained from Africa have been perpetuated ("Segregation persists, defies solution", *The Commercial Appeal*, July 9, 2015). Since most Ebonics-speakers' parents learned speech and language by listening to Ebonics-speaking caretakers, Ebonics is maintained -- on and on and on. Secondly, since most Africans in diaspora do not acquire English as their "mother tongue", they speak Ebonics as their native language or "mother tongue", fluently. Actually, enslaved Africans were forbidden to attempt to formally learn this thing called English while they were chattel slaves, and reportedly, as early freed slaves, also (Douglass, 1962, p. 79).

"Mahmee, wee bee plaeyin baaskihtball reeuh gud."[Mommy, we are playing basketball real good.] (Personal communication, Josiah Redmond Taylor, 1998, when he was two years old)

The fact is, Blacks have been denied the equal opportunity to learn English as a second language as far back as slavery time, and as recent as 1996 (Wiley, 1997, p.16). Blacks in America may learn to speak English fairly well, but having acquired Ebonics as their primary language, their ability to speak English with ideal competency will probably leave a lot to be desired. The fact is, Ebonics is there -- twenty-four, seven— seven days a week, three hundred-sixty-five days a year, so beautifully, richly African—so coveted by many other races, some of who attempt to imitate Ebonics as often as possible; or, as in the case of comedian, Jerry Seinfeld, Ebonics and its true native speakers are just plain and simply admired. Seinfeid stated the following as a guest on The Steve Harvey Show:

> "I've always had a thing for Black people. I like Black people....I love how Black people talk....I like the words that they use that I didn't know ... like 'let the window down'.. ., 'cut the light on'...., and 'put on brakes'...." (Seinfield, on the Steve Harvey Show, July 19, 2015).

"Mahmee, I dohn't haab noh paeypuh?"[Mommy, do I have any paper?] (Personal communication, Josiah Redmond Taylor, 1998, when he was two years old)

Many have foretold that *Introduction to Ebonics* will become a standard by which others will know what Ebonics is in the United States of America, and what is not Ebonics. After modestly arguing against such a prophecy, I have learned to accept this: If it is judged as a standard, then, it is so ordained. If it is so ordained, then, just as He has "no respect of persons", Providence, deductively, has no respect of languages. Question: If He has not, how can anyone else elevate himself/herself to that Position, of judging Ebonics to be much less of a relexified language than is the English language that Caucasian speakers use in this country? If I had the liberty to call such a person as he/she is, somewhere in the long list of eye-opening, strong adjectives would be the word "ignant". For only ignorance, or worse, could allow arguments against the realness of Ebonics to continue (O'Neil, 1998, pp. 38-47). "As in the past, today's negative pronouncements on Ebonics reveal a serious lack of knowledge about the scientific approach to language analysis as well as galling ignorance about what Ebonics is (more than 'slang') and who speaks it"(Smitherman, 2000, p. 53).

"Mahmie, om/um yoh baeybee?" [Mommy, am I your baby?] (Personal communication, Josiah Redmond Taylor, 1998, when he was two years old)

When I realized the importance of this Work, I often wondered, "Why was I, a no-name, given this writing Task?" The answer was in the perusal of the works of those who have written noteworthy works on Black Language, but who have failed to tell the more complete, freeing truth: The "true" language of Blacks in America "contains structural remnants of certain African languages even though the vocabulary is overwhelmingly English" (Asante, 1990, p. 22). That's the bottom line from which most linguists, scholars, "researchers in language variations", distinguished professors of English, politicians and educators shy away.

After my eyes were opened to the truth about slavery, language, and Ebonics, I was plagued by the fact that, for some reason, even many Black academicians appear to run from the truth: Some "know good and well" they understand that Black folks' language is not English-based, but they continue to choose to be proud of being called merely dialect users of the English language. They revel in the continued neglect of Black students, who are viewed as nonstandard, dialectal speakers of English.

A more liberating stand would be to say it loudly, that descendants of enslaved Africans in diaspora speak a language that is not a dialect of the English language (Smith, 1998). Many Black academicians reject the Afrocentric viewpoint, that Blacks speak a language that is based on African language structures, but that uses English words. Now, however, I have learned to accept that I was chosen for the very reason many Black academicians have refused to embrace Ebonics as a movement. They stand to lose everything. I have nothing to lose—no position, no high standing in somebody's university, no memberships in prestigious social clubs, no fear of losing grant monies for my department—little ole me who is not fearful of the backlash against which such an Africological stand would spark said, "Here am I; use me to write the message in a Book. (See Appendix III to understand the weight of naming this Work.)

"Whuht choo tahin baut, Mahmee?" [What are you talking about, Mommy?] (Personal communication, Josiah Redmond Taylor, 1998, when he was two years old)

Ebonics is not BE, AAE, AAVE, and neither is BE, AAE, or AAVE Ebonics. Repetition of that sentence is of paramount necessity. *Introduction to Ebonics, Volume I* provides a written text that can be used by educators, researchers, speech/language pathologists, parents, students, resource banks, and all to learn about true Ebonics, and then inform others about it—what it is, and what it is not. It is no wonder that the general public is unsure of what Ebonics entails, when those who have studied speech and language, and those who have made careers out of working in communication and communicative disorders do not understand what it is, or do not want to accept what it is. I am referring to those members of the American Speech and Hearing Association (ASHA), the members of the National Black Association for Speech-Language and Hearing (NBASLH), and the members of the Linguistic Society of America (LSA) many of whom insist on referring to Ebonics as BE or AAVE.

Any reference to Ebonics as a dialect of English is "unscientific nonsense". For a person to refer to Ebonics as a dialect of English when he or she knows better is, seemingly, asinine. An often heard rebuttal question made by those who view the term Ebonics as merely a synonym for BE or AAVE is this: "What's in a name, anyway?" Another often expressed question they pose is: "Why does it perturb the Africologists so much that we are choosing to continue to call the language of Blacks in America BE or AAVE?"

Here are some answers to those questions: Firstly, there is an irrefutable, scientific basis for the use of the word Ebonics that does not exist for the appellations BE, BEV, or AAVE. Secondly, 'there is power in a name', as is evidenced every time the name BE is used, deceptively, as a name for Ebonics: In a negative sense, the term BE has the power to keep most Black students enslaved to inappropriate English teaching methods that will, in turn, keep them limited English proficient. Research shows that this may lead to their continued failure or, at best, mediocre performance in school. Later, this may equate to low wage paying jobs, or unemployment and, ultimately, their being confined to the lower, socio-economic strata of American society. For many, final, ominous endings may be prison or an early grave (Tatum, 2006).

On the flip side, the name Ebonics has so much positive power that the mere utterance of its name causes the world to wonder after it. As shown by the media frenzy in December of 1996, the name Ebonics makes politicians and reporters attempt to kill it in its tracks. Why is that? What is the real fear? Once Black folks' language is accepted as an African language and not English (whether it is called Ebonics, "Pan-African Communication Behaviors" or "African Language Systems"), a new wave of respect and acceptance will flow toward Ebonics speakers. Is that the hung-over fear? That the snide remarks about the backwardness of Ebonics speakers will be forced to cease? Is that the fear? Will a pride in the creativity of Blacks in the invention of this new African Language System result? Will Blacks feel proud to be identified with it or connected to it, as they push, further, to learn English as a second language, and to make sure others learn it? Are those the fears? They will be relieved to know that their past relatives and forbearers were not untamed savages. The fact is, enslaved Africans developed and perpetuated Ebonics, a new language that others, many times, still covertly and overtly covet. To continue to refuse to call Ebonics a language other than English, is to border on being classified as *non compos mentis*.

"Daaddy gohin wihd uhs?" [Is Daddy going with us?] (Personal communication, Josiah Redmond Taylor, 1998, when he was two years old)

So far, I have hesitated to call ASHA and NBASLH out for accountability. However, I cannot continue to quietly watch Black babies, children, and teenagers being demeaned, belittled and denigrated by the school systems in this country. There are scores of children who are being allowed to drift through school with language and speech patterns that are of such a strong African accent or such strong retentions that errbady know (everybody knows) that difficult days lie ahead for them as Ebonics speakers. Employment marketability will probably be limited. That is, *ain't nohbiydee gohn wannuh hi uhm* (no one is going to hire them). I hear these students with my trained ear; I inquire about them to get a feel for their educational standings, i.e., "are they performing on grade level?"

Most times, a trained ear isn't even necessary to detect the strong use of Ebonics. These are the students who do not qualify for speech and language services for many reasons, one of which is that they would not qualify for the services, per the standardized test scores. The fact is, nowadays, these, so-called, standardized tests, e.g., *The Goldman–Fristoe Test of Articulation,* take into account what are considered to be nonstandard English or Black dialect differences. While the scoring of these tests is intended to prevent Black pupils from being mis-diagnosed as children with speech disorders, related to anatomical and physiological etiologies, these tests do not qualify Black children for speech and language development services to address their clearly discerned, so-called, nonstandard English or Black dialect anomalies. In other words, it is only the scoring of these tests, and not the tests themselves, that has changed.

I concur with the finding made by U.S. District Court Judge Charles W. Joiner in the Ann Arbor "black English", "black vernacular" or "black dialect" case, *Martin Luther King Junior Elementary School Children et al., vs. Ann Arbor School District,* (1979). In his Memorandum, Opinion and Order, Judge Joiner stated that:

A major goal of American education in general . . . is to train young people to communicate both orally (speaking and understanding oral speech) and in writing (reading and understanding the written word and writing so that others can understand it) in the standard vernacular of society. The art of communication among the people of the country in all aspects of people's lives is a basic building block in the development of each individual. Children need to learn to speak and understand and to read and write the language used by society to carry on its business, to develop its science, arts and culture . . . . (1979, p. 2)

Decades have passed since Judge Joiner wrote those words. As a speech/language pathologist, I believe, as other Africologists do, that it is the failure of the American public schools to teach Black children the necessary English language speaking and literacy skills, which has contributed to the disproportionate high school dropout rate. Consequently, this has been an ongoing epidemic of unemployability for Blacks. In my view, it is a crying shame that Black students are, many times, seemingly, *given* the high school diplomas without the English language speaking and literacy skills that they should possess. One thang's for sho, if the general public (including many, many Black people) views these students as 'not being able to talk a lick', potential employers sholl ain't goan wannuh have them haf-representin they companies and businesses, based on an inability to speak "the King's English". Yes, this is why there is such a documented high rate of unemployment among Blacks in America, stemming back to the emancipation of enslaved descendants of African origin without desensitization and education. That stem has grown into a red oak tree: In the majority of Black homes, English is still not the primary language that is spoken.

For instance, everybody knows this scenario: The evening news comes on, and, following a horrendous event, somebody has to be interviewed to relate what really happened. Many Black people make this comment: "They awwaeys gaattuh pick duh mohs noh-tawkin fohks off duh street tuh tell whuh happint." (For example, view the following: https://www. youtube.com/watch?v=zGxwbhkDjZM. This person just happened to be in the right place at the right time, and she was rewarded by notoriety afterwards, which seldom happens. Her everyday use of Ebonics made the commonly used phrase, "Aine nohbaady gat time fuh daat!" [No one has time for that!] a household saying.) I used to be one of those embarrassed folks who wondered about the news commentators' choices of interviewees. Now, I record them for data collection. I appreciate the beauty of the Black sounds emitted from their vocal apparatuses. I want to find them and hear their stories, especially about their educational experiences, and about their family members' successes and failures in the classroom. They probably all think they speak English, too. (An aside: In any major city in the U.S. that has a high crime rate of Black offenders, how many of the perpetrators can read and write fluently using English? That's just a question for thought.)

For another picture of the realness of Ebonics use in today's society, during a recent visit to a school district's human resources office, I took the liberty of jotting down parts of an unidentified, Ebonics-speaking, Black woman's loud and public cell phone conversation to which all were privy who were within earshot of her conversation. The following are some of her statements:

> *"Whihn daey come ovuh duh house?"*
> *(Translated: "What time did they come over?")*
> *"Yoh mahmah sump'en euhls wid huhsehf!"*
> *(Translated: "Your mother is amazing.")*
> *"Aine gohn wuh wihd huh, doh!"*
> *(Translated: "I am not going to worry with her, though.")*
> *"Put daat baak up unnuh dehuh!"**
> *(Translated: "Put that back under there!")*
> *"Nye, gih choh juice!"**

(Translated: "Now, get your juice!")
"Aine fih'ihn tuh plaey wih tchoo!"*
(Translated: "I am not about to play with you!")
"Gihd in naeyuh."*
Translated: "Get in there.")
"He gaat sihnse nuhff tuh sehy daat."*
Translated: "He has enough sense to say that.")
"Dihs chiyle noh he kihn eet."*
Translated: "This child has a hearty appetite." (9/28/2015)
*(These are statements the woman made to her, reportedly, grandson, who was with her.)

Since those were actual words spoken by the woman, I do not want to hear anyone tell me that Ebonics is dying out. She had her grandson with her, and she mentioned a whole lot of references to people with whom she deals everyday – neighbors, doctors, children, children's friends. I thought to myself, "There is a whole world of similar Ebonics speaking folk right at her house – in her community." Such treasures I hear every day. So, do not tell me that Ebonics is converging into English. Her conversation is one of many such conversations that I hear while out and about each day. These are conversations of Black people speaking their mother tongue, Ebonics. I know the language in an intimate way because Ebonics is my mother tongue, also.

That is where ASHA and NBASLH come in. Many suggest that it is time for ASHA and NBASLH to rewrite their policies and guidelines concerning Ebonics. Time is of the essence. As a speech and language pathologist whose native language or mother tongue is Ebonics, I firmly believe Ebonics is, in fact, a relexified African language, and not a social dialect of English. I firmly believe that when a speaker of any language, who is not proficient in English, 'exhibits speech and/or language anomalies that are attributable to endogenous or exogenous etiologies, that are biophysical or anatomical in nature, or even when the speech or language anomalies have no known etiologies, he is manifestly communicatively handicapped in his native language. That is, the speech and/or language anomalies he exhibits are native language speech and/ or language defects, deficits or disorders'.

Therefore, I believe that, just as there are limited English proficient speakers of Cambodian, Chinese, Italian, Korean, Russian, Spanish, Vietnamese and all other languages, who are truly communicatively handicapped when they exhibit speech and/or language anomalies that are disorders, defects or deficits, this also applies to speakers of African languages. That is, when limited English proficient speakers of African languages exhibit speech and/or language anomalies, these speakers of African languages are truly communicatively handicapped. Likewise, when limited English proficient speakers of Ebonics exhibit speech and/or language anomalies, these speakers of Ebonics are, also, truly communicatively handicapped. That is, the speech and/or language anomalies that Africans and speakers of Ebonics exhibit are speech and/or language deficits, defects or disorders that are not attributable to Niger-Congo African or Ebonics grammar rules.

As a speech and language pathologist (SLP) whose native language or mother tongue is Ebonics, I have the following concern: There are no tests or assessment tools available to evaluate and differentiate the truly communicatively handicapped speakers of Ebonics from the limited English proficient Ebonics speakers, whose limited English proficiency is actually intrusions, interference modifications, or transfer phenomena retained from their mother tongue. Ultimately, when I went to the ASHA web page seeking ASHA's view on speakers of Ebonics who might have truly communicative handicaps as bilinguals, I discovered that, in 1984, ASHA had created a section entitled "Position Statement on Clinical Management of Communicatively Handicapped Minority Language Populations". This Position Statement was adopted following, "what is believed to have been, one of the most extensive development and review processes ever undertaken in the creation of an Association position statement". In its extensiveness, however, ASHA failed to mention the names of any such minority language populations, except Spanish. I believe ASHA could have, at least, made a footnote mention of the view held by many researchers, that Ebonics is an African language system. That would have been professionally fair, since there are two major schools of thought on Ebonics: 1) researchers who deem Ebonics to be a dialect of English, and 2) researchers who deem Ebonics to be an African language. Concerned clinicians should ask ASHA: "What's up with that?"

However, I, still, strongly urge speech and language pathologists, who are sincerely interested in becoming more effective in their service delivery to speakers of Ebonics, to utilize the information provided by ASHA under this section of the ASHA web page. For the fact is, with those Ebonics-speaking clients in mind as members of a non-English "minority language population", ASHA's position Statement on Clinical Management of Communicatively Handicapped Minority Language Populations" dictates the following: "Assessment and intervention of speech and language disorders of limited English proficient speakers should be conducted in the client's primary language." For speech and language services providers who do not have the staff that meets the competencies for assessing or working with limited English proficient speakers, namely, for purposes in this Book, limited English proficient Ebonics speakers, they must adhere to ASHA's "Alternative Strategies for Use of Professional Personnel" outlined in "Clinical Management of Communicatively Handicapped Minority Language Populations".

As I further consulted the ASHA website for ASHA's position on truly communicatively handicapped bilinguals, I found more information under the heading "Position Statement Social Dialects Committee on the Status of Racial Minorities", and the subheading "Implications of the Position on Social Dialects". Wisely, ASHA had included a question and answer section. The following is the answer to one of the frequently asked questions: "Does the position paper have implications for our professional role with bilingual populations?" Dr. Lorraine Cole, then Director of ASHA's Office of Minority Concerns, provides ASHA's reply:

> Yes to a limited extent. A bilingual speaker may present a situation that is analogous to a speaker who uses a social dialect. The bilingual speaker may mix the phonological and grammatical rules of the minority language with those of standard English (and/or nonstandard English). Similar to social dialect speakers, bilingual individuals speak English, but may do so with linguistic rules that are different or nonstandard. The rules used by the bilingual speaker can be attributed to the rules of the minority language spoken and to the community in which he/she lives. (ASHA, 1985)

As a directive to SLPs regarding their professional role with bilingual populations, the Director of ASHA's Office of Minority Concerns goes on to state:

> The position statement has similar implications for bilingual individuals as it does for other nonstandard English speakers. If the bilingual individual seeks to acquire more standard production of English, the speech-language pathologist may provide elective services. However, as stressed in the position statement, a particular language base is required including a thorough understanding of the linguistic rules of both languages. (ASHA, 1985)

Concerning bilingual individuals who exhibit a speech or language disorder in their dominant language, the Director of ASHA's Office of Minority Concerns states:

> For the bilingual speaker who exhibits a speech or language disorder within his or her dominant language, speech or language intervention would be indicated. It should be stressed, however, that a comprehensive evaluation by a knowledgeable speech-language pathologist is required prior to initiating treatment. Considerations for providing assessment and treatment to the bilingual communicatively handicapped are under study by the ASHA Committee on the Status of Racial Minorities. (ASHA, 1985)

Notice that the Director of ASHA's Office of Minority Concerns states that: *"For the bilingual speaker who exhibits a speech or language disorder within his or her dominant language, speech or language intervention would be indicated"*. However, ASHA's Office of Minority Concerns Director stresses that *"a comprehensive evaluation by a knowledgeable speech-language pathologist is required prior to initiating treatment"*. In my view, as speakers of an African language, and not a social dialect of English, 'for the bilingual speaker of Ebonics who exhibits speech or language disorders within his or her dominant language (Ebonics), speech or language intervention would be indicated'. Likewise, viewed as speakers of an African language, for bilingual speakers of Ebonics, "a comprehensive evaluation by a knowledgeable speech-language pathologist is required prior to initiating treatment". Clearly, viewed as an African language, which it is, ASHA's discussion of the speech or language disorders of Ebonics speakers would be more appropriately addressed under ASHA's website entry on "Clinical Management of the Communicatively Handicapped Minority Language Populations".

In essence, except *as* a footnote on page 9 in the ASHA website under the heading, "Position Statement Social Dialects Committee on the Status of Racial Minorities", and the subheading "Implications of the Position on Social Dialects", there is no mention of Ebonics made at all. The ASHA footnote that does contain the word Ebonics reads as follows:

> Some Black professionals prefer to use the term Ebonics instead of the more popularly used term Black English. Derived from the words *ebony* and *phonics,* the term Ebonics is intended to avoid the focus on race and emphasize the ethnolinguistic origin and evolution of this variety of the English language. ("Position Statement on Social Dialects", ASHA, 1983)

"What! ASHA's inference that the term Black English is a synonym for the term Ebonics, to some, is repugnant. Under the heading "Position Statement on Social Dialects", a chronology of the development and preparation of ASHA's Position Statement is provided. In this chronology, a disclosure is made that a Position Paper was prepared by ASHA's Committee on the Status of Racial Minorities. It is also disclosed that the initial draft of ASHA's position paper was submitted by the Committee on the Status of Racial Minorities to ASHA's Legislative Council, and that in 1982 ASHA's Legislative Council, unanimously, approved the Position Paper.

This chronology of the development and preparation of ASHA's Position Statement on Social Dialects makes it clear that as far back as 1982 ASHA's Committee on the Status of Racial Minorities and ASHA's Legislative Council knew fully and well that, as originally coined by its author, the word Ebonics is a portmanteau of two words, i.e., ebony and phonics. Just as ASHA knew that, as originally coined, the word Ebonics is a portmanteau of the words ebony and phonics, ASHA knew fully and well that, when the term Ebonics was coined as originally defined, the word Ebonics did not refer to a variety of

English. Yet, ASHA has, seemingly, elected to mislead its membership by positing and propagating the fraud that the word Ebonics refers to a variety of English. This next statement may be offensive to some, but it is necessary to offend sometimes: Reportedly, to some of the linguists and researchers who view Ebonics as an African language, and not a dialect of English, the claim by ASHA, that *"the term Ebonics is intended to avoid the focus on race and emphasize the ethnolinguistic origin and evolution of this variety of the* **English** *language" is as white supremacist bilge."*

Similar to ASHA, NBASLH, also, has a position on Ebonics. NBASLH's position is viewed by some Africologists to be even more beguiling than the position of ASHA. The older leaders of NBASLH know that the word Ebonics refers to an African language system, and not a Social Dialect of English. I know this because, in 1991, when I was a graduate student, I attended my first NBASLH National Convention that was held in Los Angeles, California. It was at that Convention that I heard the term Ebonics mentioned for the first time. I was converted that weekend because I had already begun questioning the origins and development of Black speech and language. Dr. Ernie A. Smith, linguist, was the keynote speaker at that Convention. Need I say more? No, I do not. But, I do want to thank NBASLH for allowing Dr. Smith to evangelize that weekend. Afterwards, I contacted Dr. Smith, and he took me under his tutelage. Even after twenty-four years of talking and conferring with him, many nights until the wee hours of the morning, what I have learned about the speech and language of Black folks in America can fit into a thimble in comparison to what he has sought to teach me from his knowledge base. Ebonics as a subject is far-reaching and vast.

After reading through the book, *History of the National Black Association for Speech-Language and Hearing (NBASLH): The First Twenty Years, 1978-1998*, written by Mr. M. Eugene Wiggins (2014), I had to put it down for a minute. Mr. Wiggins is a giant in the world of NBASLH, and in the field of speech and language pathology. He likened the term Ebonics and the Oakland California School Board's use of it in its 1996 Resolution to a "cancer". At first, I was livid with anger that he would write such. Then, that changed to sadness that he has such a closed mind to the Africological essence of Ebonics. How could I be angry with a man over his choice of theoretical leanings? My concern is that Mr. Wiggins' reference has the potential to leave a lasting, negative impression on anyone, especially a new student in the field of speech/language pathology, who may not have ever read anything else about Ebonics. Such a first impression would deter the future clinician from fully understanding Ebonics. A lack of understanding that Ebonics is, in fact, a non-English language that has some speakers who are truly communicatively handicapped could, in turn, diminish the quality of the future services offered by that clinician, because of his/her attitude toward Ebonics-speakers. Presently, ASHA's and NBASLH's views of Ebonics, that it is a "nonstandard social dialect of English", aligns Ebonics with the deficiency model as a dialect of a minority population whose speakers are only entitled to elective speech/language pathology services.

Mr. Wiggins also stated the following: "Williams' creation of the term did not tie it to West Africa with the assertion that it, not English, was our native language" (p. 46). Negative! For the actual words of Dr. Williams concerning the creation of the word Ebonics and its tie to West African origins, see *Ebonics: The True Language of Black Folks*, Williams, 1975, p. 100. (See, also, Chapter Two in this Book, "Ebonics: Re-claiming and Re-Defining Our Language" by Dr. Williams.) The entire true Afrocentric and scientific understanding of Ebonics is predicated on African languages being established as the grammatical base of Ebonics. Using my experience as a speech-language pathologist, I must admit that my appreciation for the speech and language of Blacks deepened when I accepted the scientific findings of the origins of Ebonics; I went above ASHA's admonition that 'clinicians have a thorough knowledge of the linguistic rules of the non-standard English speaker'. I, actually, hungered for a more thorough knowledge of the linguistic rules of Ebonics. This new attitude toward Ebonics allowed me to view the Ebonics speaker in a more positive light, and I offer services in a more positive light. All in all, I hope that the condition of "cancer" that Mr. Wiggins, metaphorically, calls Ebonics was as all-consuming as Mr. Wiggins claims it was, and that it will continue to spread until it has permeated every cell of every living person's brain in the world.

To not belabor the point: ASHA and NBASLH have the ball in their courts. May the spirit of the first NBASLH Convention held in Chicago, Illinois, May 5-6, 1970, ignite again, and may NBASLH flourish as never before, as it remembers that the Black community needs it more now than ever before. Throughout America, school board policies need to be rewritten, so that Ebonics-speaking students are respected and served as needed. Or you know what? All of them who say "no" to such a suggestion should pull off their false faces and hoods and stop pretending they care about the Black child being 'left behind'. On the other hand, if the answer is a majority-ruled, resounding "let's show that we really care about equal educational opportunities for the Ebonics-speaking Black student", one place to start is to address the inability of many Ebonics-speaking students to communicate orally in an effective way because it has the potential to impact their educational success in the long run. For, as stated by Judge Charles Joiner earlier above, "Children need to learn to speak and understand and to read and write the language used by society to carry on its business".

How can Ebonics-speaking children learn, unless they are taught or served? Who can teach or serve them best? Those who are proficient in Ebonics and/or those who understand the intricacies of Ebonics can teach them. Understanding Ebonics is relevant to the education of the Ebonics-speaking Black children, even those children who have speech and/or language disabilities.

4

ETYMOLOGICALLY AFRICAN

African Oral Literature is the historical and geographical shadow of our people. Whether African or otherwise, oral literature is perhaps as old as humanity itself. Where the people are, there they have with them their oral literature: it is not locked up in crowded libraries, it is not hidden in dusty archives, instead, it is inscribed in the heart and mind of the people, ever ready to flow out their lips like an ever gushing spring of water. It binds together the entire people, from the youngest to the oldest -- it belongs to them, they belong to it.

-- John Mbiti, *African Oral Literature* (1966, p. 246)

Commonly used words in the United States of America that have authentic African beginnings

Explanatory Notes

Before there were Ebonics words, there were African words. The beginning convergence of African words between African ethnic groups, began, possibly, before the slave traders' descents upon Africa, but, assuredly, that was a pivotal point of mixing. I write that by permission. Contrary to popular teachings, African slaves had strong African-based languages when they were captured, enslaved, and transported to various parts of the world. Common sensibly, in the bows of the various ships during the Middle Passages, these languages were used as the Africans attempted to comfort each other, support each other, and make some kind of sense out of their obvious, tragic positions. I fail to even begin comprehending the width and depth and height of their despair, as they laid in each other's sweat and blood and tears and urine and defecation and vomit and disease and infestations of parasites. Surely, these intelligent people didn't ride in the bows of those ships and not begin a mode of communication some kind of way -- with their separate lexicons but similar bases. Somebody among them had to offer words of encouragement or songs of hope. If nothing else, in my "sanctified imagination", I believe that singing and humming was utilized. Because they held onto that 'Something within them' during the rough times of extreme hunger, extreme cold, extreme heat, and extreme states of disease, even though, reportedly, "over 10 million died as direct consequences of the Atlantic slave trade alone", millions, also, survived. (See http://www.africanholocaust.net/html_ah/holocaustpecial.htm#fact.)

The system of slave trading was demeaning and cruel; we often forget that many nations indulged in this crime against the African nations -- from the Netherlands to Britain to Spain to France to Portugal to Cuba . . .. Multitudes upon multitudes of Africans were enslaved. "Africans can rightfully call the inhumane act the African holocaust where approximately 15-50 million Africans lost their lives from 1482 to 1888" (Blackshire-Belay, in Crawford, 2001, p. 172).

In reference to U.S. Ebonics-speakers, however, the words listed below attest to the fact that there is an African, lexical content in the language of slave descendants of African origin in America, and, therefore, there is an African content in English: Reportedly, "hundreds, perhaps thousands of words from Afrika survive in Ebonics". Kimani Nehusi cited researchers as Turner, Cassidy, Warner-Lewis, and Allsopp as sources whose works attest to this. (Nehusi, in Crawford, 2001, p. 99) Some of the entries below are mainstays in the lexicon of English. This is only a minuscule reporting of the much larger number of African lexical items that currently exist in America. This chapter gives the researched etymologies or African languages from which these words derived. The words will be presented using the following format: 1) The familiar, adopted spellings or forms of the words as used in English; 2) the original African country of origin, along with the African orthographical representation or form of the word in that language, when found; 3) a brief definition or meaning; and 4) a reference.

ETYMOLOGY AND DEFINITIONS

ankh [Egypt - *aŋk*]; a cross having a loop for the upper vertical arm and serving esp. in ancient Egypt as an emblem of life. (Budge, 1969; Webster, 2009, p. 49)

bad [Mandingo/Bambara - *a ka ny; ko-jugu*]; positive to the extreme (Majors, 1994)

banana [Wolof]; elongated, most times, tapering fruit with soft pulpy flesh enclosed in a usually yellow rind (Webster, 2009, p. 95)

banjo [Kimbundu]; a musical instrument consisting of a drum-like body, a long fretted neck, and four or more strings that are strummed with the fingers (Webster, 2009, p. 96)

biddy [Kongo; Angola - *bidi'bidi*]; a bird (Turner, 1949, p. 63); a young chicken (Webster, 2009, p. 119)

bro [Mandingo - *brer*]; elder brother (Holloway & Vass, 1993)

bookoo [Yoruba - *buku*]; to increase, to bless (Turner, 1949, p. 69)

chimpanzee [Tshiluba - *kivili-chimpenze*, translated "mockman" or "ape"]; an equatorial African ape, allied to the gorilla but much smaller, more arboreal and less fierce (Webster, 1979; Webster, 2009, p. 215)

cola [Malinke - *kolo*]; Coca-Cola, a trademark: a carbonated soft drink colored usually with caramel and flavored usually with extracts from kola nuts. Kola nuts are the bitter, caffeine-containing chestnut-sized seed of a kola tree, an African tree (Webster, 2009, p. 242, 692)

cootie [Malay - *kutu*]; body lice (Turner, 1949)

dashiki [Yoruba - *dansiki*]; a usually bright colored loose, fitting pullover garment (Webster, 2009, p. 316)

dodo [Yoruba]; empty (i.e., an empty-headed person) (Turner, 1949, p.76)

doodoo [Ewe - *du du*]; to fall off, to leak (Turner, 1949, p.78)

ebony [Egypt]; a hard heavy blackish wood . . .(Webster, 2009, p. 393)

fag or faggot [Egypt - *fagit*]; refers to an Egytian goddess . (Budge, 1978, p. 260)

fuck [Wolof - *fut*]; to be nude; to have sexual intercourse. (Turner, 1949, p. 193) Note: This may explain why the American black male speaks this word with passion as no other—"mother fucker"—it stems from the enslaved African man having to submit to the knowledge that the slave owners were having forced sex with the enslaved African woman— his children's mother—or his own mother—or his brothers' children's mothers. . . They were being constantly raped by the slave masters. Just food for thought. .

goober [Bantu, akin to Kimbundu - *nguba*]; peanut (Webster, 2009, p. 538)

gumbo [Bantu - akin to Umbundu *ochinggombo* okra]; a soup thickened with okra pods or file and containing meat or seafoods and usu. vegetables: okra (Webster, 2009, p. 556)

jive [Wolof - *jev*]; swing music or the dancing performed to it or glib, deceptive, or foolish talk (Webster, 2009, p. 673)

juju [Hausa/Yoruba]; "a fetish, charm, or amulet of West African peoples; the magic attributed to or associated with jujus; a style of West African music that is characterized by a rapid beat, the use of percussion instruments, and vocal harmonies" (Webster, 2009, p. 677)

Kwanzaa [Swahili - *matunda ya kwanza*]; translated, "first fruits of the harvest first fruits"; created in 1966, specifically, as an African holiday by Maulana Karenga.

Lordy, Lord [Mandinka - *la'ila*]; translated, "oh, God!" (Turner, 1949, p. 120)

marimba [akin to Kimbundu - *marimba*-xylophone; Angola]; a xylophone of southern Africa and Central America with resonators beneath each bar (Webster, 2009, p. 759)

mumbo jumbo [Mandingo]; some Mandingo peoples of the western Sudan, a priest believed to have power to protect his village from evil. 2) An object believed to have supernatural powers; a fetish. 3) confusing or meaningless activity; unintelligible incantations; obscure ritual. 4) Gibberish. [*ma-ma-gyo-mbo*, "magician who makes the troubled spirits of ancestors go away": *ma-ma*, grandmother + *gyo*, trouble + *mbo*, to leave.](American Heritage Dictionary, 1981, p. 862)

Neggur [Egyptian]; the goose-goddess who laid the sun-egg; (Budge, 1978, p. 398.)

Neggur {Egyptian}; In Shabaka and Smith's book, *Nigger A Divine Origin* (2003), the following is offered as an explanation of how the Black people of ancient Kemit (Egypt) were known as Kemits, as well as NGRS or niggers. They state:

> . . .[J]ust as there are people today who worship Jesus Christ as their Lord and Savior, and as such call themselves Christians, in ancient Kemit there were people who worshipped the God Nger-s and the Goddess Neggur. As such, these people called themselves NGRS and were known as NGRS. . ... [J]ust as many of the people who lived in ancient Kemit were also known as Semitic people, those

in ancient Kemit who worshiped the god NGRS were also called Nigritic people and were known as both Kemitic and Nigritic people. (p. 31) . . . In ancient civilizations, such as Ethiopia, Babylon and India, there were NGRS or Nigritic people who lit the torch of pre-civilization thousands of years ago. In Ethiopia they were called Nagran People. In Babylon they were called Ngirri people. In ancient India they were called Naga people. (p. 32)

NGR {Egyptian}; According to Budge, 1978, Mercer, 1993 and Gardiner 1927, the ancient writing system used by the Egyptians did not entail the use of vowels. Therefore, for thousands of years, in ancient Egyptian or Kemitic hieroglyphics, the root word NGR was written on temples and pyramids, in consonants only. An entire book is needed to delve into the ancient writing system used by the people of ancient Kemit with the absence of the use of vowels. Succinctly, in *Nigger A Divine Origin* (2003) Shabaka and Smith state:

> . . .[I]n the ancient Kemitic language, it is the root word NGR that is the origin and etymology of the word Niger.. . .[T]he original homeland of the people who were known as NGRS was the 'Equatorial Lakes source of the Nile', the Southern source of the Nile being Lake Victoria in Uganda where it flows North and junctures with the Blue and white Niles in Sudan, then on into the Mediterranean in Egypt. . . . [T]he people who are the NGRS of West and Niger-Congo Africa or Nigritia have their historical origins or roots in and are descended from the NGRS of Eastern Nigritia or ancient Kemit (Egypt). (pp. 14 – 15)

The root word NGR existed in the ancient Egyptian sacred writings or hieroglyphics, i.e., the mdw ntr. It is attested as being in the mdw ntr 4000 years before any evidence of a Latin civilization even existed. Therefore, the Latin language could not be the language base of the word *niger or ngr*. (p. 18)

nigger [Egyptian] A present day "appellation of offense and yet a term of endearment among many people of Niger-Congo African ancestry", making "it incumbent on scholars of Niger-Congo African or Nigritic descent to pierce the Euro-centric veil of secrecy" to see why "the English language lexicographers may not be willing to, or do not feel obliged to delve beyond Latin or the Romance languages for the origin and true meaning of the word nigger" (Shabaka and Smith, 2003, p. 8). Shabaka and Smith further state:

> . . .[W]hile the word nigger has a negative connotation in some European dictionaries and among many descendants of enslaved Niger-Congo African people today, long before the word nigger became part of the European lexicon, the root word niger was in usage in ancient Kemit dating back to at least 4000 B.C. I maintain that, by using the recognized method of comparative philology and etymology, when a careful and critical analysis is made of the word nigger, consistently one will find the word identifying ancient gods and goddesses of Kemit (Egypt) as well as people who viewed themselves as Nigritic or Nigritian people. (Shabaka and Smith, 2003, p. 8)

okay [Wolof, Djabo, Mandingo]; alright (Holloway & Vass, 1993)

voodoo [Ewe - *vodu*]; a spirit (good or bad) intermediary between God and man; to bewitch by or as if by means of voodoo (Webster, 2009)

yam [Wolof]; [Fulani - *nyami*]; translated "to eat"; a moist usu. orange-fleshed sweet potato (Holloway & Vass, 1993) (Webster, 2009, p. 1450)

yo [Mende]; yes. [Hausa]; a reply by villagers to a call. . . (Turner, p. 187)

you know "*Uno*"; - reportedly, purely African in origin (Holloway, 1993)

zebra [probably a Congo language]; any of several fleet African mammals . . . related to the horse but patterned in conspicuously stripes of black or dark brown or white or buff (Webster, 2009, p. 1455)

5

RELEXIFICATION

In the study of language in schools, pupils were made to scoff at the Negro dialect as some peculiar possession of the Negro which they should despise rather than directed to study the background of this language as a broken-down African tongue -- in short to understand their own linguistic history, which is certainly more important for them than the study of French Phonetics or Historical Spanish Grammar.

-- Carter G. Woodson, *The Mis-Education of the Negro*, 1933, p. 19

The deep phonology of Niger Congo African languages retained in adopted European words and phrases

Explanatory Notes

How many times has an English teacher drilled over and over to his/her Black students who speak Ebonics (especially, southern Mississippi, Tennessee, and Arkansas Ebonics- speaking students) that they are being sloppy when they say "dis" for "this"; or that it is incorrect to say "moh" for "more"; or that they are speaking poor English when they pronounce "last" as "las", etc.? How many have heard a teacher tell a student, "You are not going to talk like that in here"? These pronunciations attest to the fact that there must be something to the prevalence and high frequency of the sounds that are being emitted from their Black minds as speech. These speech patterns resound over the U.S., day after day; North, South, East and West. In this chapter, the words illuminate the phonetics ("the inventory and structure of the sounds of speech", O'Grady, et al., 2005, pp. 15-56) and phonological ("the function and patterning of sounds", O'Grady, et al., 2005, pp. 57-109) rules that are 'retained substratum (deep structural) mainstays in the, overall, grammar system of Blacks in the U.S., based on the Niger-Congo and Bantu language systems' (Clegg, 1998, p. 3; Blackshire-Belay in Crawford, p. 182).

After these truths are provided, no longer should the misconception, that Blacks speak a dialect of English, be accepted. That myth is far from the truth. American Blacks have been "born into, reared in, and continue to live in linguistic environments that are different from Euro-American English-speaking people" (Smith, 1998, pp. 54-55), and, historically, the way Blacks talk has lasting roots, 'like a tree planted by the water'; Black language 'shall not be moved'.

It is possible to become familiar with the following examples of some of the major, highly predictable, systematic phonological rules that many Blacks use: [This information, though technical for the average reader, helps lay a necessary foundation for the reader's, overall, understanding of Ebonics.]

1. Facts prove that, as a linguistic continuation of Africa in America, while the voiced dorso-velar, nasal continuant /ŋ/ does occur as

a word final, single phoneme, i.e., in words as thing and string, it is not distributed as a suffix morpheme for construction of the progressive tense in English, i.e., ringing.

2. In Ebonics, the voiced retroflex or velar spirant /r/ is phonotacticly restricted -- which explains, in part, the nonoccurrence of the voiced retroflex or velar spirant /r/ as a word final consonant in the words "more", "door", and "floor". They become "moh", "doh", and "floh", respectively. (See Smith, *The Africanist-Ethnolinguistic Theory, 1994.*)

In regard to the production of consonant cluster configurations, they are also made according to the rules of the West, Niger-Congo, and Bantu African languages from which Ebonics is derived. 'Word final consonant cluster configurations either do not occur at all, or occur in very restricted patterns.' (Welmers, 1973, p.3)   For instance, la*st* becomes las; ho*ld* becomes ho*l*; ha*nd* becomes ha*n*; and buil*d* become buil. (See Smith, *The Africanist-Ethnolinguistic Theory*, 1994, for more information.)

Even though it does not take a scholar to acknowledge that, comparatively speaking, the speech of Black people sounds differently from the speech of Caucasians, this chapter was written to visually account for some of these differences. This chapter lays the foundation of a beginning point in the development of a written language for Ebonics, using, mainly, the English alphabet followed by the IPA transcriptions of those words as spoken by the Ebonics speaker. Hyphens are used in the Ebonics pronunciations to indicate syllabic divisions; Pronunciations are indicated between brackets ([]), following the entry word. The symbols used are listed in the chart under the heading "IPA Rudimentary Pronunciation Key". A high-set mark / ' / is used to show primary or acute stress or accent in the IPA transcriptions. Broad versus narrow transcriptions are used. The alphabet of the International Phonetic Association (IPA) was used, also, as the unbiased authority to help portray these differences.

In *Introduction to Ebonics . . .*, for a better understanding, just as the IPA System denotes one alphabet to consistently represent one vowel sound, the Taylor Orthographic System of Ebonics Spelling will utilize one or two English alphabets to represent each vowel sound, while using the consonants that are used in English; however, the Ebonics speaker will use the retained African mode of pronunciation. For instance, it is truly amazing to hear an Ebonics speaker from Mississippi or Tennessee using his native tongue's sound system while reading a passage that is clearly written in English (Simpkins, 2002), i.e., "The dog went down the street" might be read as "Duh dog wihnt down duh skreet".

While this chapter includes a representation of the many, *commonly* used words by Blacks and Euro-Americans, by no means is this list all inclusive; also, definitions are not included, since Stylistics is comprised of the words in Ebonics and English that **share** definitions – the sound system is not shared, but the definitions are shared. Also, again I stress that most of the pronunciations are based, mainly, upon Southern dialectal variations of Ebonics, as used by many Blacks, mainly in Mississippi, Tennessee and Alabama. Although that statement is being issued to account for and acknowledge that there are varieties of dialectal variations of speech, even within Ebonics, a linguistic rule is a linguistic rule; North, South, East, or West, Blacks share rules for combining sounds to shape and form words, and they share rules for arranging the words to express complete thoughts -- straight from their original homeland-- Africa. So, a Northern speaker of Ebonics may incorporate many "northern" variations to his or her Ebonics that relate to the Northern dialect that true Euro-American English speakers use, but that same Northern speaker of Ebonics will share a basic grammatical structure with the Southern speaker of Ebonics, the Western speaker of Ebonics, and the Eastern speaker of Ebonics. Reportedly, too, "the majority of Africans landed in the southern states" {Asante, 1990, p. 23}, which means that, even though many Blacks later moved "up" East or "out" West, their United States linguistic roots may be traced to Mississippi, Tennessee, Arkansas . . . . Or is that deductive reasoning unsound? Why would anyone be ashamed of that bit of Southern Ebonics heritage?

As the reader may have gathered, much fine-tuning is needed in the development of a written style of Ebonics; it was decided, however, that the more closely Ebonics was written using the current English spellings of words, the better would be the flow of the reading and understanding of the entries in *Introduction to Ebonics*.

*The Taylor Orthographic System of Ebonics Spelling© (TOSES) was devised as a new writing system that incorporates a broad transcription system to distinguish the way one Ebonics word sounds from the way other Ebonics words sound. Only a high set or acute accent mark was used throughout this chapter. The English alphabet was used to designate the unique structures of each word. TOSES basically spells words as they are presented when spoken by the average speaker of Ebonics, particularly, Southern Ebonics. Consistency was sought in using the various phonological rules while depicting each word's orthographic representation. TOSES establishes bare minimum pronunciations.

IPA RUDIMENTARY PRONUNCIATION KEY

(Based on the symbols used by Robert J. Hall, Jr. in *Linguistics and Your Language* [1960])

VOWELS Symbols	Key Words	Phonetic Definitions
a	far	Low central unrounded
æ	at	Low front unrounded
ɑ	pot	Low back, slightly rounded
e	cake	High-mid tense front unrounded
ɛ	bed	Low-mid lax front unrounded
ə	sofa	Low-mid lax central unrounded
i	tea	High tense front unrounded
I	it	High lax front unrounded
o	oatmeal	High-mid tense back rounded
ɔ	bought	Low-mid lax back rounded
u	boot	High tense back rounded
U	book	High lax back rounded
Λ	cut	Low-mid tense central unrounded

CONSONANTS

Symbols	Key Words	Phonetic Description
b	bib	Voiced bilabial plosive stop
č	church	Unvoiced palatal assibilate stop
d	did	Voiced apico-alveolar plosive stop
ð orđ	there	Voiced inter-dental fricative
f	fief	Unvoiced labio-dental fricative
g	gag	Voiced dorso-velar plosive stop
ğ or ǰ	judge	Voiced palatal assibilate stop
h	hat	Voiced glottal aspirate
j	yes	Voiced palatal glide
k	kick	Unvoiced dorso-velar plosive stop
l	lead	Voiced alveolar lateral
ł	full	Voiced guttural lateral
m	madam	Voiced bilabial nasal continuant
n	no	Voiced aveolar nasal continuant
ŋ	sing	Voiced dorso-velar nasal continuant
p	pipe	Unvoiced bilabial plosive stop
r	roar	Voiced retroflex velar spirant
s	sauce	Voiceless alveolar sibilant
š or ʃ	shush	Unvoiced palatal sibilant
t	tight	Unvoiced apico-alveolar plosive stop
Ө	think	Unvoiced inter-dental fricative
v	valve	Voiced labio-dental fricative
w	wow	Voiced bilabio-velar glide
	where	Unvoiced labio-velar glide
z	zebra	Voiced alveolar sibilant
ž or ʒ	measure	Voiced palatal sibilant

TAYLOR SYSTEM RUDIMENTARY
PRONUNCIATION KEY

VOWELS

Symbols	Key Words	Phonetic Description
a	far	Low central unrounded
aa	at	Low-lax front un-rounded
ah	pot	Low-mid-lax back rounded
aey	cake	Mid-tense front un-rounded
eh	bed	Mid-lax front un-rounded
uh	sofa, cut	Low-mid-lax central un-rounded
ee	tea	High tense front un-rounded
ih	it	High lax front un-rounded
oh	oatmeal	High mid-tense back rounded
aw	bought	Low-mid-lax back rounded
oo	boot	High tense back rounded
u	book	High lax back rounded
iy	dry	low central fronting
au	loud	low central backing
oy	joy	low back fronting

Each entry consists of 1) the Taylor Orthographic System of Ebonics Spelling; 2) the International Phonetic Alphabet Transcription; and 3) the English Orthographic Spelling

CONSONANTS

Symbols	Key Words	Phonetic Description
b	**bib**	Voiced bilabial plosive stop
ch	**church**	Voiceless palatal affricate
d	**did**	Voiced apico-alveolar plosive stop
dj	mea**s**ure	Voiced palatal sibilant
f	**f**ie**f**	Unvoiced labio-dental fricative
g	**gag**	Voiced dorso-velar plosive stop
h	**h**at	Voiceless glottal aspirant
j	**j**u**dg**e	Voiced palatal assibilate stop
k	**k**i**ck**,**c**ut	Unvoiced dorso-velar plosive stop
m	**m**ada**m**	Voiced bilabial nasal continuant
n	**n**o	Voiced alveolar nasal continuant
ihn	sing**in**	Voiced apico-alveolar nasal continuant
l	**l**ead	Voiced alveolar lateral
p	**p**i**p**e	Unvoiced bilabial plosive stop
r	**r**oa**r**	Voiced retroflex velar spirant
s	**s**au**c**e, **c**ity	Voiceless alveolar sibilant
sh	**sh**u**sh**	Unvoiced palatal sibilant
t	**t**igh**t**	Unvoiced apico-alveolar plosive stop
th	**th**ink	Unvoiced inter-dental fricative
f	ba**th**room, ba**th**	Unvoiced labio-dental fricative
d	**th**e, ei**th**er	Voiced dental fricative
v	**v**al**v**e	Voiced labio-dental fricative
z	**z**ebra	Voiced dental sibilant
w	**w**o**w**	Voiced bilabio-velar glide
wh	**wh**ere	Unvoiced labio-velar glide
y	**y**es	Voiced palatal glide

Reflexification

A

aa [æ] I

'aab-straack or 'aab-skraack
[æbstræk] [æbskræk] abstract

aack [æk] act

'aaf-duh [æfdə] after

aaf-duh-'noon [æfdənun]
afternoon

'aag-guh-vaeyt [ægəvet] aggravate

aan, aeyn or ihn [æ] [en] and

aank-pihn [enkpɪn] ink pen

'aa ohn noh ['æ ono] I don't know

aap [æp] apt

aey [e] hey

'aey-buh [ebə] able

aeyn/ aeyn't [ein] [eint] am not, is
(are) not, does (do) not

aeyn noh [eino] there is no

'ah-guh ['ɑ gə] argue

ahm [ɑm] arm or I'm (See *uhm*)

'aw-duh ['ɔw də] ought to, order

'aw-fuh ['ɔ fə] off of,offer

aw-'iyt [ɔ 'aɪt] all right

awl [ɔl] oil

'aw-mohs ['ɔw mos] almost

B

baaf [bæf] bath

'baaf-room [bæfrum] bathroom

baan [bæn] band

'baauh [bæə] bear

'bah-bee-kyoo [bɑbikyu]barbecue

'bah-duh [bɑdə] bother

baut [baut] about

beeaans [biæns] being as since

bee-'foh [bifo] before

beh-chuh [bɛčə] I'll bet you

'behd-uh [bɛdə] better

beh-ih-'naht [bɛɪn'ɑt] better not

behs [bɛs] best

'bihl [bɪəl] build

bleeve [bliv] believe

'bleev-ihn [blivɪn] bleeding

blohn [blon] belong

bohd [bod] board

bohf [bof] both

'bohf-uh [bofə] both of

bohne [bon]born

boh-'reht [borɛt]barrette

'boo-dee-fuh [budifə] beautiful

boof [buf] booth

boo-koo [buku]beaucoup

brang [bræŋ]bring

brehf [brɛf] breath

'bruh-duh [brʌdə]brother

'buh-buh guhm [bʌbəgʌm]
bubble gum

'buh-duh [bʌdə] butter

'buhf-day [bʌfde] birthday

bu [bʌs] bust

byoos [byus] abuse

C

cehp [sɛp] except

chaeynse [čens] chance

chawl [čɔl] you all (following a
word that ends with [t])

chehch [čɛč] church

choh [čo] your (following words
that end with [t])

choo [ču] you (following words

that end with [t])

chuhch [čʌč] church

'chuhl-uhn [člən] children

D

daat [ðæt] that

'daat-uh-waey [ðætəway] that way

daey [ðe] they

daeyns [dens] dance

'daey-uhns [ðeəns] theirs

'dahl-luhs [dɑləs] dollars

dak [dak] dark

dee-'claa-uh [diklæə] declare

deef [dif] deaf

deese [ðis] these
dehf [dɛf] death

dehs [dɛs] desk

'deh-sehs [dɛsɛs] desks

'deh-uh or **'daa-uh** [ðeə] [ðæə]
there or dare

deh-uh aeyn't [ðeəent] there ain't,
there is not

'dehv-uh [ðɛvə]devil

dihm [ðɪm] them

dihn [ɖɪn] then

dihs [ɖɪs] this

dihs-uhn [ɖɪsən] this one

'dihs-uh-waey [ɖɪsəwe] this way

dihs-'kraak [ɖɪskræk] distract

dihs-'traak [ɖɪstræk] distract

'dih-uhnt [ɖɪənt] didn't

doe or **doh** [do] door

dohn-noh [dono] don't know

doh s [ɖoz] those

dohs [doz] doors

draw [drɔ] drawer

draws [drɔs] drawers

'drehk-lee [drɛkli] directly

drihmp [drɪmp] dreamt

duh [ɖʌ] the

'duh duh [ɖəɖə] the other

duh-'mah-ruh [ɖə 'mɑ rə] tomorrow

duh-'uh-duh [ɖəʌɖə] the other

'duhn-iht [ɖʌnɪt] did it

E

eech [ič] itch

'eech-ihn [ičɪn] itching

'eed-nihn [idnɪn] evening

'ee-ihn [iɪn]eating

'ee-kuh-tuh [ikətʌ] equal to

'ee-uhm-mohs [iʌmos] even most

'eh-biy-dee [ɛbaɪdi] everybody

'eh-baa-dee [ɛbædi] everybody

'eh-ree [ɛri] every

'eh-ree-thaang [ɛriθæŋ] everything

eht [ɛt] ate or at

eh-uhse [ɛəs] else

eht [ɛt] at

ehz [ɛz] as

Euhl [ʌl] Earl

F

faack [fæk] fact

'faam-blee [fæmbli] family

'faan-guh [fæŋə] finger

faas [fæs] fast

faa-uh [fæə] fair

fah or fuh [fɑ][fə] for

'fa-ihn ['fɑ ɪn] farting

'fahl-lihn [fɑl ɪn] following

'fahl-luh [fɑl ə] follow

'fam-uh [fɑm ə] farmer

'faw-dee [fɔdi] forty

fawk [fɔk] fork

fawght [fɔt] fault

fawse [fɔs] false

fawt [fɔt] fault

'Fehb-ee-yeh-ree [fɛbijɛri]
  February

'fih-dee or fihf-dee [fɪdi][fɪf di]
  fifty

'fih-ihn uh [fɪnə] fixing to
  (about to)

'fihn-tuh [fɪntə] fixing to

(about to)

'fih-uhn tuh [fɪəntə] fixing to
  (about to)

fih-'teent [fɪtint] fifteenth

'fih-uhls [fɪəs] fields

fiy [fai] fire

fiyn [fain] find

'fiy-uh [faiə] fire

'fiy-uhd [faiəd] fired

floh [flo] floor

fluhsh [flʌš] flesh

'fluhs-kraey-dihd [flʌskredɪd]
  frustrated

foh [fo] four or before

fohf [fof] fourth

fohk [fok] folk

'foh-teen [fotin] fourteen

frihn [frɪn] friend

froh [fro] afro

fruhm [frʌm] from

fuh [fʌ] for

'fuh-duh-moh [fʌdəmo]
  furthermore

fuh-giht [fəgɪt] forget

fuhs [fʌs]first

'fyoo-nuhl [fyunəl] funeral

G

gaad [gæd] got

gaat [gæt] got, has

gad [gad] guard

gaf [gaf] golf

'gah-bihch [gɑbɪč] garbige

'gah-dihn [gɑdɪn] garden

'gah-uhn [gɑən] garden

gehs [gɛs] guest

gih, 'gih-uh [gɪ] [g ɪə] give

gihd 'awf [gɪdɔf] get off

'gih-mee [gɪmi] give me

giht [gɪt] get

gohn [gon] go on or is gone

gohn [gon] is/are going to

'gohn-nuh [gonə] is/are going to

graayn-'chihl-uhns [grænčɪləns] grandchildren

grehd [grɛd] great

'grohm-moh [gromo] grandmother

'groh-shrees [grošris] groceries

'gub-nuh [gʌbnə] governor

guh or guhl [gʌ] [gʌl] girl

'guhn-nuh [gʌnə]is/are going to

gwiyne [gwain] going to

gwiyn-tuh [gwaintə] going to

gwohn [gwon] go on

H

haab [hæb] have

haad-duh [hædə] had

haaf-tuh [hæftə] have to

haa ihn uh [hailnə] how in the

haap-puhnt [hæpənt] happened

haa-uh [hææ] hair

had or hahd [had] [hɑd] hard

haeyn [hen] hand

haeyn-chuh [henčə] handkerchief

hahl-lihn [hɑlɪn] hollering

'hahsh-pih-tuh [hɑšpItə] hospital

hat [hat] heart

heep-uh [hipə] heap of, lot of

'heh-uhm [hɛəm] heaven

hehf [hɛf] health

hehp [hɛp] help

hehsh [hɛš] hush

hihm [hIm] hem

hih-suhn [hIsən] his

hih-uh [hIə] here

hih-uhd [hIəd] heard

hiy come [haikəm] how come

hiy-dee doo-dee [haididudi] how are you?

hiy-'doo [haidu] how do you do?

hiy muhch [haimʌč] how much

hiy yoo [haiyu] how are you

hoh-lohn [holon] hold on

hohl [hol] hold

hohn-gree [hongri] hungry

hohpe [hop] help

hoys [hois] horse

huh [hʌ] her

huhd [hʌd] heard

huh ihn [hʌIn] hurting

huhn [hʌn] her's

huh-rup [hʌrʌp] hurry up

I

I'ihg-nuhnt [Ignənt] ignorant

ihm [Im] him

'ihm-buh-lohpe [Imbəlop] envelope

ihm-'pah-tuhnt [IImpətənt] important

ihn [In] end

'ihn-juhn [Injə̂n] Indian, engine

'ihn-tee baa-dee [Intibædi] anybody

iy-iyt [aIaIt] alright

iys [aIs] I'm

iy ohn noh [aIono] I don't know

'iyuhn [aIən] iron

J

jah [jɑ] jar

jaeyk [jek] jerk

'Jaeyn-yee-eh-ree [jæn j ɛ ri] January

jehj [jɛj] judge

jehs [jɛs] just, jest

K

kah [kɑ] car

kaht [kɑt] cart

'kah--uhn [kɑən] cotton

kehch [kɛč] catch

kehk [kɛk] cake

'keh-uh [kɛə] care

'keh-uh-fuh [kɛəfə] careful

kihn [kɪn] can

'kih-uht [kɪət] killed

'kiy-nuh [kainə] kind of

klawf [klɔf] cloth

klihnt [klɪnt] cleaned

klohz [kloz] clothes

koh-'koh-luh [kokolə] coca cola

kohl [kol] cold

kohs [kos] coast

koht [kot] court

kohn [kon] corn

'kohn-brehd [konbrɛd] cornbread

'koh-nuh [konə] corner

'koo-puhn [kupən] coupon

'krees-tuhn [kristən] christian

'kuhd-nuh [kUdnə] could not have

'kuh-duhnt [kUdənt] couldn't

kuhm-'mih-uh [kʌmɪə] come here

'kuhm-oh or **'kuhm-ohn** [kʌmo]/ [kʌmon] come on

'kuhmp-nee [kʌmpni] company or accompany

kuhn-fuhnce [kʌnfəns] conference

'kuh--uhn [kUən] couldn't

kraws [krɔs] across

krien [kraɪn] trying

krien [kraɪn] crying

kruhs [krʌs] trust

kriy [kraɪ] try

'kuh-ihn [kʌɪn] cousin

'kuh--ihn [kʌɪn] cutting

'kuh-lihn [kʌɪn] coloring

kuhse [kʌs] curse

kwiy [kwaɪ] choir

L

'laab-ruh-toh-ree [læbrətori] laboratory

laak [læk] like

laas [læs] last

'laeyd-lee [ledli] lately

lahne [lɑn] learn

Lawd [lɔd] Lord

laws [lɔs] lost

lehb-uhn [lɛbən] eleven

lehd-dihsh [lɛdɪš] lettuce

'lehd-iht [lɛdɪt] let it

lehf [lɛf] left

lehk-trihk [lɛktrɪk] electric

'leh-mee [lɛmi] let me

'leh-mee-lohn [lɛmilon] let me alone

'lehs-see [lɛsi] let's see

'liy-behr ee [laibɛri] library

liyd uh [laidə] lighter

lihf [lIf] lift

lihs [lIs] list

'lih-uh [lIə] little

lohw 'daun-ihs [lodaunəs] most lowdown

luhs [lʌs] lust

M

maai [mæi]/[mai] my

'ma-buhs [mɑbəs] marbles

'maa-suh [mæsə] master

'mae-ehd [mæəd] married

maeyn [men] man

'maeyn-chun [menčən] mention

maey-kaeyse [mekes] make haste

'maey laak [melæk] made like, pretended

maey-tuh [metə] tomato

mauf [maUf]mouth

meh-bee [mɛbi] maybe

'meh-sine [mɛsɪn] medicine

'mihm-buh [mɪmbə] remember

'mih-uk [mɪək] milk

'miy-kuh-waeyve [maikəwev] microwave

'miy-naeyse [mainəs] mayonnaise

miynes [mains] mine

miyt-'neh-uh [maitnɛə] mighty near/close to

miyn [main] mind

moh [mo] more

'moh-ihn [moɪn] more than

moh-nihn [monɪn] morning

mohs [mos] most

'muh-cee [mʌsi] mercy

muh-'dih-uh [mʌdɪə] mother dear

'muhd-uh ['muhv-uh[mʌdə]/ [mʌvə] mother

'muhnk-ihn [mʌnkɪn] monkeying

muhnt [mʌnt] month

muhs [mʌs] must

'muhs tuh [mʌstə] must have

N

naa [næ] now

naaa [næ] no

'nah cheht [nɑčɛt] not yet

nah 'meen [nɑmin] do you know what I mean

'naay-uhn [næən] none; not one (See "naey-uhn".)

'naa-nuh [nænə] banana

'naa-ree [næri] not hardly

'naa-chuh-lee [næčəli] naturally

'naa-truhl [nætrəl] natural

'naey-uhn [neən] none; not one (See "naay-uhn")

naw [nɔ] no

nawf [nɔf] north

'naw-suh [nɔsʌ] no sir

'need-nuh [nidnə] need not

'neent [niənt] need not

'neh baut [nɛbaUt] nearly about

'nehb-uh, nehv-uh [nɛbə]/[nɛvə] never

nehks [nɛks] next

nihm [nɪm] them

niy or**'niy-uh** [nai]/[naiə] now

'noh baa dee[nobædi] nobody

nohd [nod] knew

noh 'hau [nohaU] no way

nohm [nom] no ma'am

noh 'ree-uhn [noriən] no reason

nuff [nʌf] enough

nuh [nə] the, nor

'nuhm-uh [nʌmə] number

'nuhn-uh [nʌnə] none of

nuhs [nʌs] nurse

'nuh-tihn [nʌtɪn] nothin

'nuh-uhn [nʌən] nothing

nuh-'uhn [nʌən] no I didn't

'nuh-nehg [nʌnɛg] nutmeg

O

oh-'kree [okri] okra

ohl [ol] old

ohm or **uhm** [om]/[əm] I'm

'oh-ma or **'uh-muh** [omə]/['ʌmə]
   I'm going to

ohn [on] on

'oh-vuh [ovə] over

P

'paan-nees [pænis] panties

paeyn [pen] pan

'paeyn-sehs [pensɛs] pants

'paeyn-chuhn [penčən] pension

'paey-puh [pepə] paper

paeys [pes] paste

'pah-daey [pɑde] party

pahk [pɑk] park

'pah-suhm [pɑsəm] opossum

paht [pɑt] part

'pah-taey [pɑte] party

'pee-chuh [pičə] peach

'pee-puh [pipə] people

'pih-duh-fuh [pɪdəfə] pitiful

pihn [pɪɪn] pen

poh [po] poor

pohk [pok] pork

'poh-lees [polis] police

pohnt [pont] point

'poh-shuhn [pošən] portion

'pohs tuh [postə] supposed to

poh-ʻtehk [potɛk] protect

ʻpoh-shuhn [pošən] portion

ʻprah-blee [prɑbli] probably

ʻprah-blee-uhll [prɑbliəl] probably will

priyz [praɪz] pry

puh-ʻfeh-suh [pəfɛsə] professor

puh-ʻleez [pəliz] please

ʻpuh-puhs [pʌpəs] purpose

Q

ʻkwah-duh [kwɑdə] quarter

ʻkwahn-uh-dees [kwɑnədis] quantities

kwawt [kwɔt] quart

kwuhs-tuhn [kwʌstən] question

R

raat [ræt] right

ʻraas-slihn [ræslɪn] wrestling

ʻraav-uh [rævə] rather

ʻraey-joh [reĵo] radio

ree-ʻmehm-uh [rimɛmə] remember

ʻreh-kuh-lehk [rɛkələk] recollect

ʻreh-dee-oh [rɛdio] radio

ʻreh-gluh [rɛglə] regular

ree-ʻmehm-uh [rimɛmə] remember

rehch[rɛč] reached

ʻrih-buh [rɪbə] river

ʻrih-uh [rɪə] real

rohse [ros] rolls

S

ʻSaad-ee [sædi] Saturday

ʻsaa-kuh-fiys [sækəfais] sacrifice

saang [sæŋ] sing

sahs [sɑs] source

ʻsah-shish or ʻsah-shie [sɑšɪš]/ [sɑšɪ] sausage

saht [sɑt] sat

ʻsaht uhp [sɑtʌp] sat up

sawf [sɔf] soft

ʻsaw-tuh [sɔtə] sort of

seed [sid] saw

ʼseemp-liyk [simplaɪk] seemed like

sehb-uhn [sɛbən] seven

seht [sɛt] sit

seh [sɛ] say

'shaad u(p) [šædəp] shut up

shahp [šɑp] sharp

shawt [šɔt]short

sheht [šɛt] shut

sheh-vuh [šɛvə] shovel

shoh [šo] sure

'shoh-duh [šodə] shoulder

shohl [šol] sure

shoh-laey [šole] surely

shoh-'nuhf [šonʌf] sure enough

'shud-nuh [šUd nə] should not have

sih-chee-'yaey-shuhn [sɪčiješən] situation

sihn [sɪn] send

sihns [sɪns] sense

sih-chee-'yaey-shuhn [sɪčiješən] situation

skaeyse [skes] scarce

skahf [skɑf] scarf

skehd [skɛd] scared

skjoos [skjus] excuse

skoh [sko] score

skraap [skræp] strap

skrahp[skrɑp] strap

skreet [skrit] street

skrehnt [skrɛnt] strength

skrihk [skrɪk] strict

skwehz [skwɛz] squeezed

slah-bihn [slɑbIn] slobbering

slehp [slɛp] slept

snuck [snʌk] sneaked

sohl [sol] sold

soh or soh-uh [so]/[soə] sore

sohze [soz] so as

'spaa-uhns [spæəns] experience

'spaa-uh [spæə] spare

spehk [spɛk] expect or respect

splaeyn [splen] explain

spoom [spum] spoon

staan [stæn] stand

staank [stænk]stink

stahd [stɑd]start

staht [stɑt] start

'stihd-uh [stIdə] instead of

'stehd-uh [stɛ dəh] instead of

stoh [sto] store

stohm [stom] storm

stoh-ree [stori] story

straak or **skraak** [stræk]/[skræk] strike

straach [stræč] scratch

straeyng [steŋ] string

strahp [strɑp] strap

strehnt or **skrihnt** [strɛnt]/[skrInt] strength

suh [sʌ] sir

suhb-traak [sʌbtræk] subtract

suhch [sɛč] search

suh-'fohs-tuh [sʌfostə] supposed to

'suhmp-uhm [sʌmpəm] something

suhm-'teet [sʌmtit] something to eat

suhm-'whaa-uh [sʌmʍæə] somewhere

'sus-tuhs [sUstəs] sisters

swaw-uhd [swɔəd] sword

swoh [swo] swore

'swoh-dehd [swodəd] swelled

T

t'aeynt [tent] It's not

taey-kih-sloh [tekIslo] take it slow

taeynch [tenč] a small amount

taeyn-chuhn [tenčən] attention

taeys [tes] taste

'taey-uh [teə] tail

'tah-buh [tɑbə] tolerable

tahl-uh-buh [tɑləbə] tolerable

'ta-tuh piy [tetəpaI] potato pie

taw-ihn bau [tɔInbaU] talking about

tawt [tɔt] touched

tee-juhs [tiĵəs] tedious

teef [tif] teeth

tee-niyn-chee-'wee-nee [tinaičiwini] tiny

tehch [tɛč] touch

tehs [tɛs] test

'teh-sihs [tɛsIs] tests

tehch [tɛĉ] touch

thaang [æŋ] thing

thaank [θæŋk] think

thoh uhp ['θo ʌp] throw up

thoht or **thohk** [θot]/[θok] throat

thohw [θo] throw

thoo [θu] through

'tihn-chuhnv [tɪnčən] attention

tihn tuh [tɪntə] attend to or tends to

tiyd [taid] tired

tohs [tos] toast

tohd iht [todɪt] told it

toh [to] tore

tohl [tol] told

tohn [ton] torn

toof [tuf] tooth

triyn [train] trying

triyn nuh [trainə] trying to

troof [truf] truth

'truh-buh [trʌbə] trouble

truhs [trʌs] trust

tuh [tə] to

'tuh-duh [tʌdə] the other

tuh-'gehd-duh [təgɛdə] together

tuhnt [tʌnt] turned

U

uh [ʌ]/ [ə] a, of, or

uh [ʌ] used as an interjection

uh-'boh-shun [əbošən] abortion

uh-'bruhp [əbrʌp] abrupt

'uh-duh [ʌdə] other

'uh-duh-wiyz [ʌdəwaɪs] otherwise

uhf-lee [əfli] earthly

uh-'gihns [əgɪns] against

uh-'juhn [əǰʌn] adjourn

uh-'loos [əlus] loose

'uh-duhn [ʌdən] other one

'uhm uhm uhm [ʌmʌmʌm] well, you don't say?

uhm 'uhn [ʌmʌn] not so

uhnnn [ʌn] good gracious

uhn um [ʌnʌm] good gracious

uh-'traak [ətræk] attract

'uh uhl [ʌ ʌl] trouble is brewing

'uh uhl naa [ʌʌlnæ] big trouble is current

um [ʌm] I'm or them

um [ʌm] arm

ummm [ʌm] somebody is in trouble

'umn umn [ʌmʌmn] no

'um uh [ʌmə] I'm going to

um-uh-'rehl-luh [ʌmərɛlə] umbrella

'un-kuh [ʌnkə] uncle

'un-nuh [ʌnnə] under

uv[ʌv] of

uv-um [ʌvəm] of them

V

vuh-'nehl-uh [vənɛlə] vanilla

vawt [vɔt] vault

vehs [vɛs] vest

W

waeys [wes] waste, waist

'wah-duh [wɑdə] water

'wah-luh [wɑlə] water

'wah-luh mel-on [wɑləmɛlən] watermelon

waw [wɔ] war

waws [wɑs] wasp

'weh-cuhm [wɛcəm] welcome

wehk [wɛk] work

wehp [wɛp] wept

whaa-uh or waa-uh ['ʍæə]/[wæə] where

'whih-chuh or 'wih-chuh [ʍɪčə]/ [wɪčə] which

whihn or win [ʍɪn]/[wɪn]when

whiysor wiys [ʍais]/[wais] while

whuh or wuh [ʍʌ] [wʌ] where

whuhs-'up or wuhs-'up [ʍʌsʌp]/ [wʌs ʌp] what's up

whup or wup [ʍʌp]/[wʌp] whip

whut or wut [ʍʌt]/[wʌt] what

wid-it ['wɪdɪt] with it

wihd [wɪd]with

wihd-uh ['wɪd ə] with a

wihd-uhm ['wɪ dəm] with them

wihf [wɪf] with

wihf-uh [wɪfə] with a

wihn [wɪn] wind

wine [wain] whine

wiy [wai] why

wiy [wai] wire

wiyl [wail]wild

wiyt [wait] white

woh [wo] wore

wohnt [wont] want

wom [wom] warm

wuhd [wʌd]word

'wuh en [wʌən] wasn't

wuhf-fuh [wʌfə]worth

wuhk [wʌk] work

wuhl [wʌl] world

wuhs [wʌs] worse

wuh-shup [wʌšəp] worship

wuh-som [wʌsəm] worrisome

wuz [wʌs] was

'yaan-duh [jændə] yonder

yaas [jæs] yes

'yaas-suhm [jæsəm] yes ma'am

'yaas-suh [jæsə] yes sir

yahd [jad] yard

yall [jɔl] you all

yeh-bout [jɛboU] nearly about

'yeh-stih-dee [jɛstɪdi] yesterday

yoh [jo] your

yoh [jo] to call someone or to say
   yes

yohs [jos] yours

yuhng-uhns [jʌngənz] young ones

'yood uh bihn [judʌbɪn] you would
   have been

'yoh-uhn [joən] yours

Z

'zaa-muhn [zæmən] examine

zaa-muh-'naey-shuhn
   [zæmənešən] examination

Y

TWELVE COMMANDMENTS

FOR TEACHING

AN EBONICS-SPEAKING CHILD

Empirical evidence has proven all these words to be truth, words that were permitted by God to be spoken by Africologists, people who have studied the "true language of Black folks".

I. EBONICS is the linguistic tradition that was brought out of Africa by West Africans, Niger-Congo Africans, and Bantu Africans, when they were captured and held in bondage in the wilderness of North America for over "two hundred and forty-six" hundred years. These Africans were one hundred percent (100%) whole male and female people, created in God's image, who spoke true African languages.

II. Thou shalt hold no other language, i.e., English, French or Irish, as the phonological, morphological, semantical and/or syntactical base, or total grammar base, of EBONICS.

III. Thou shalt hold no language as superior; for truly, all languages are, self-evidently, equal, including the most "neo-African language", EBONICS.

IV. Thou shalt not use the name of EBONICS by the name Black English or African American English or Afro American English or American Black English or Black English Vernacular or Black Vernacular English, for Black English or any other appellation referring to English in reference to EBONICS is a false image that attempts to make the grammar base of EBONICS something other than a genetically African language, a language that was created out of necessity by enslaved Africans. Thou shalt not bow down thy intelligence to English—nor attempt to force others to serve English as anything other than the **lingua franca** that it is.

V. Thou shalt not take the name EBONICS, vainly, for it was created by a qualified psychologist and approved by dedicated scholars, linguists, psychologists, and academicians, after careful consideration of the descriptive and prescriptive aspects of the speech and language patterns of African Americans.

VI. **Remember** that African Americans are Africans in diaspora, scattered away from their native country. Their language has not converged more into the English language. For two hundred forty-six years, Black people were held in abject isolation from the slave owners and overseers. Today, yes, even today, the living areas for the majority of African Americans remain segregated, which accounts for the following: 'There is no dialect that African Americans speak that is based on a German grammar system, using African words;' the sound system of EBONICS exhibits unique and similar qualities to African languages; the consonant-vowel configuration is peculiar from the English language; most words are shared between EBONICS and English, but many meanings are different; many words, phrases, idiomatic expressions, and sayings that African Americans use are peculiar to them, **alone**. EBONICS is predictable, systematic, legitimate and rule-governed.

VII. Honor and respect an EBONICS-speaking child as being a 100% human being—and his father—and his mother.

VIII. Thou shalt not kill the EBONICS-speaking child's spirit by demeaning his culture and language, or by misdiagnosing his normal language as substandard or some type of pathology.

IX. Thou shalt not commit plagiarism by using the term EBONICS to mean anything other than an African-based language system.

X. Thou shalt not continue to attempt to steal the African heritage of the language of most African Americans from them. _Under a genetic classification of languages, the linguistic system of EBONICS is not English; it is African._

XI. Thou shalt not bear false witness against those who advocate equal educational opportunities for EBONICS-speaking children.

XII. Thou shalt not covet any Black person's speech; neither his gesticulations, nor his oratorical skills, nor his artistry, his music and dance, culinary skills, nor anything that pertains to Blacks in the Diaspora.

"Peace and Blessings."

APPENDICES

APPENDIX I

AN ANTHOLOGY OF DEDICATIONS

Ms. Exermena Redmond: My grandmother was my heart—and I was hers. "You look jehs lack yo granmama" was something I did not want to hear—but it was true. Still look like her—ack like her—tawk like her—real "down home" Ebonics-style when I want to—'cause she was my second, primary child caretaker—and her native tongue was EBONICS—as is mine. If only I had known then that "Gromo's" speech was African- based and not just embarrassing "bad" English. …

Ms. Geraldine Taylor: My mother-in-law used Ebonics fluently, AND she spoke Standard American English (SAE). I mean really *spoke* it. Frank called her "Mama"; our children called her "Grams"; to me, she was my mother-friend. I appreciated her strength, love and counsel over the years. R.I.P., Ms. Mama Grams Geraldine.

Mrs. Bertha Baptist Sanford: There will never be another. She was wise, full of love, and special, cause she respected and valued every person, and they, likewise, respected and honored her: R.I.P., "Grammarian" Bertha of Como, MS: gone but never forgotten because of the legacy and the generations of Sanfords that she left behind.

Mr. and Mrs. Arlander and Willett Weathersby: No words can express the kindness they showed to me during a special period of my life. I loved them, and they loved me. R.I.P., "Pop" and Mom.

Dr. Columbus B. Hopper: The blessing of this man, a stranger, gave me the impetus I needed to realize that my pen was blessed and would enrich the lives of others. He was an angel who took the time to mark an "A" on a sociology paper that I submitted to him while a junior at Ole Miss. From his mouth, today, he has stated with authority that my "A" was the only "A" he EVER gave on this particular writing project over an expansive teaching career from which he is now retired: Four semesters per year for over twenty years . . . - imagine that honor of having the ONLY A ever given--and being remembered by your sociology professor! He is the epitome of how teachers' words "carry a lot of weight"—even after thirty-some odd years—I remember his blessing, and he remembers my paper—mutual memories. R.I.P., Dr.

Mrs. Sallie Hillard: A friend of mine, plus a whole lot more—clinical supervisor, comforter, guidance counselor...For some reason, as this book was being finished, I became misty-eyed and nostalgic as I thought about how proud Sallie would have been, just for the stick-to-abilitiness I exhibited in finishing this Project. More teachers are needed as Sallie, who accepted me for all of myself—from my Ebonics-talking self to my sensitive self, to my "needy" self from my strong, determined self—Acceptance of all of me made me want to be the best that I could be. I'm so glad our paths crossed. Rest on, Sallie. Rest on.

Dr. Gloria Kellum: She was in place at Ole Miss to keep me safely during the storms: She shielded me from racism's destructive tide. I ventured to fly, knowing she was close by.

Attorney and Mrs. Frederick and Margaret Clark: They believed in this Work over seventeen years ago. I thank them for their generosity that allowed a powerful seed to be planted.

Sister Oprah Winfrey: Fame and fortune have not made her, selectively, forget how to speak the first language she learned from her birth to five year experience, in the environment in which it was spoken and heard: Ebonics, period. Presently, being a proficient speaker of Standard American English, that she learned as a second language, helps her stay "on course" toward her end purpose of 'edifying God by serving others'.

Bishop T.D. Jakes: He preaches the Word, and, often, Ebonics is his natural tongue of delivery. Praise God for such a powerful example of how speaking Ebonics illuminates one's reason for being: to praise and serve God.

President Barack Obama; Rev. Jesse Jackson, Sr.; Dr. Martin L. King, Jr.: Great Black men who can/could speak to the masses of people, and be understood – Black masses-White masses. That makes/made them, at the very least, bilingual.

Brother Steve Harvey: I thank him for being a true Ebonics speaker who has shown the world that naturally speaking his native tongue has been a tool, used to propel him toward acceptance and wealth, as he communicates real life experiences of being Black in America. Thank you, Mr. CLO.

Mr. Jerry Seinfeld: His humor has boosted me to laughter when I was in depths of despair. When I witnessed him expressing an appreciation for the language of Black folks, I was all the way in my love for him as a real person who has real feelings for what is real: The way Black folks talk. I thank him for the lifting.

Sister Iyanla Vanzant. She makes Ebonics use alright because she uses SAE, too, when she wants to, being, unashamedly, at the least, bilingual.

Sister Nabeehah Shakir. 'Every time we look around, somebody's gone on home.' This soldier is one of the reasons why Ebonics became a household word in 1996: She gave the Oakland Unified School System the fight power to go all the way with their efforts at helping their Black student population. Her spirit of dedication is evidenced in the blurb she wrote for this book. Rest from your labor, Sister!

Raymond Bettis; Roy Coleman; Ernest Walker. God's ways and what He allows to happen leaves us dumbfounded at times. These three "brothers" of mine were here one day, and then they were gone. Enough said.

Forebearers. I wish I could write the names of the 'forty million' African people, reportedly, who did not make it to America, and elsewhere, dying in route on the slave ships during the Middle Passage. They are due homage and respect, as are the 11 million Africans, reportedly, who did make it, bringing their African language roots that held strongly, despite the influx of English words they heard for over two hundred and forty-six years.

Brother Kirk Whalum. We will forever be grateful to the LORD for having inspired Rev. (Pastor Kenneth T., Sr.) and Mrs. Helen (Whalum Rogers) to create Kirk. He is such a work-of-an-artist whose use of language has come full circle, from Ebonics to SAE, to a few more languages, transcending to the language of music. In the latter, he is so fluent that all of the peoples of the world understand what he says when he plays his saxophone. We also thank Sister Ruby for sharing him with us.

National Black Association for Speech, Language and Hearing. It is because of this organization presenting Dr. Smith as a keynote speaker in 1991 that this Book has been written. Thank God for the dedication that the members of NBASLH have in their mission of aiding all Blacks who have communicative concerns.

Mrs. Deborah Harris. She epitomizes God's gift of a supervisor to a workforce: She leads by example, making all under her adhere to being "ambassadors for peace". Period. She is the most considerate, though super-efficient, manager on this planet. You can forget it if you think 'a dog is going to hunt' outside of the realm of reasonable-ness, on her watch.

The "Canyon's" Occupants. Yes, I want to take the time to salute all of my buddies who made sure I spoke good Ebonics because that was what was spoken in the community from which I evolved. We went to school and church, and shopped in the "Canyon". Remember Shainberg's and Woolworth's? Just know that you are loved and appreciated for the shared experiences of being Black and living off Lynch Street. What a time we had. **Albenny Price. The Browns. The Fizers. The Greens and Crocketts. The Wansleys. The Binghams. The Lewises. The Womacks. The Culbersons. The Bozemans. The Beachums. The Jessie Black family; Lutee; Diddi Bop. Mrs. Ophelia Chatman and family. The Taylors. The Holmans (and Linda). The Aberdeen Street Crocketts. The Wansleys. The Aberdeen Street Crocketts. The McLaurins. The Fletchers. The Aberdeen Street Johnsons. The Lucedale Johnsons. The Browns. The Pattons. The Oreys. The Stewarts. The Andersons. The Draines. The Densons. The Sessumes. The Kings on Wiggins. The Davises on Wiggins. The Harveys. The Adams. The Uptons. The Knights. The Carters. The Mannies. The Jenkins. The West Jackson Community Youth Choir members, under the directorship of John**

Palmore, Thomas Darden, Charles Dillon, and Mr. Evans. Thanks also to five high school friends who need to be mentioned here: Laura Lee Sparkman. Lauren Campbell. Patricia Cole, Terilyn Fluker, and Phyllis Grant, Marion Pinson, Cheryl Turner, Ruby and Brenda Fizer, the Wingfield High School Class of '74, and the members of Mt. Nebo M.B. Church and Cherry Grove M.B. Church. Thanks to all of the Patriots of the Canyon, and especially Corinth, Lucedale, Macon, and Lucedale Streets, who have gone on, namely: Mr. and Mrs. Bailey (and Leslie), Mr. Eddie and Mrs. Ruby Fizer ,both deceased, (I thank them for letting us use their front porch as the meeting place. Now, looking at the size of that porch makes me realize that God was in the miracle working business even back then.) and their sons, Green, Eddie, Jr, and Johnnie, Mrs. Mason, Mr. and Mrs. Ross, Mrs. Bowie, Mr. and Mrs. Jack and Hazel Perry, Uncle Jack and Aunt Ida Perry, Mr. and Mrs. Corn, Mr. Robert Wansley, Ms. Anna, Mr. and Mrs. Adams, Mr. and Mrs. Upton, Mrs. Emma Collins, Ms. Katie Mae Taylor, Mrs. Holden, Mr. Jessie Johnson, Mr. and Mrs. Samuel and Helen Grant, Mr. and Mrs. Charles and Lauree Adams, Mr. and Mrs. Dan and Sarah Orey, Mr. and Mrs. Johnny and Annie Pearl Knight, Mr. and Mrs. Stewart, Pastor and Mrs. Fred and Grace Black, The Carrs, The Bozemans, and all those who lived and are now gone who were there between 1956 and 1974.

Brother James Spann. Over his career as a science-biology teacher, he was one who made a great impact on his students at Blackburn Junior High, showing them Black manliness, Black wisdom and intelligence, and Black pride. I thank him, even to this day, for being "all that, and a bowl of cherries". In other words: He was a super-hero teacher to us, and he prodded us to be his super-students. For that we are grateful.

Mrs. Barbara Hilliard (Blackburn Jr. High; Mrs. Gordon, Mrs. Fisher, and Mrs. Harris (Wingfield High); Mrs. Draine and Mrs. Ruth Williams (Isable Elementary). These six Black female teachers protected us; directed us; chastised us; guided us; taught us; brought us up to where we belonged; accepting our Ebonics, but modeling and exemplifying English so that we could learn it – and we did.

APPENDIX II

<u>TRIBUTES</u>

ALPHA TRIBUTE: Rev. Dr. Jessie Redmond (Daddy)

Each March 10th finds me nostalgically missing my Daddy. That was the day he died (2006). And, so, I have written his tribute in a book that has been written, partly, because of him, for I learned Ebonics while listening to him speak it. When I saw Jessie Redmond for the first time in 1956, I was a content baby. Then, he looked so mocha-chocolaty black: So, black became good because Black was my Daddy. Then, I smelled his delicious cologne: It infiltrated my nostrils. So, even now I wish I could have just one more sniff from his chest. Then, I saw his beautiful, inviting smile: So, smiling became good: Smiling was what I did in reciprocation. Then, I heard his Southern, strong, tenor-baritone-like, determined voice: So, later, I began searching for that same voice in a man. Then, I felt his strong hands holding me up: So, for forty-nine years I knew he would catch me, if ever I needed him to. Then, he taught me discipline; he reproved me; he chastised me; he corrected me as a good father does: So, I matured and grew strong because of his love. Then, he made sure he showed me the necessary nurturing that a father should. So, this set me on a right path to marry such a man as my sweet, kind-hearted, loving, strong, Christian Daddy was. Then was then, and now is now. So, now, each year, on March 10, although he had lived a good, long life for seventy-four years, it is as if he disappeared too quickly—as vapor, rushing up out of here like he was late for an appointment, but not as vapor in my mind: His love is as real now—his teachings are as relevant today—his Ebonics usage is as clear right now—as it was then. So, it is so.

OMEGA TRIBUTE

'Ain't My Mama, Mariah, Ain't She a Woman?'

My mother, Mariah Wilson Brinkley Redmond (MuDear) is "not just another woman; she's not"; she is "more than a woman" and is "every woman", for she has the astuteness of Saint Joan of Arc; she could have been a great ruler, as Hatshepsut of Egypt was; she has the will power of Rosa Parks; she has the charitable spirit of Eva Peron (Evita); she is the philosopher and theologian that Saint Catherine of Siena was; her spirit of cleanliness equates her to Florence Nightingale; she has the charm and taste of Queen Nefetari; she heeds the direction of the Holy Spirit, as did Isabella Baurnfree (Sojourner Truth, the "travelling preacher"); she has strong arms that have seen her through many work days, arms as strong as Serena and Venus Williams'; her voice is as melodic as Mahalia Jackson's; her prophetic abilities run second only to those of the biblical Anna; she shows the wisdom and generosity of the biblical Abigail; when my Daddy met MuDear, she was as pure as Mary was before she had Jesus; she loves to serve as did the biblical Martha, Lazarus' sister; she is about as industrious and giving as is Oprah Winfrey; her love for her husband was as protective and wholesomely sweet as Michelle Obama's is for hers; she would have stood by her man, if needed, as Hillary Clinton stood by hers; she is as much an Ebonics speaker as she is a Contemporary English speaker, as was Shirley Chisolm; and her love for her children is as protective as was the biblical Rachel's over Isaac: Lastly, my mother has been blessed with longevity, as was Maya Angelo. No other woman is more loved by her children as my mother is by hers. So, again I ask: "Ain't my Mama, Mariah, ain't she a woman?"

TRIBUTE TO DR. ROBERT L. WILLIAMS

"The Father of Ebonics"

When Dr. Robert L. Williams sought a true name for the language of Black folks, he was rewarded with an "epiphany"experience whereby the name "Ebonics" burst through upon a wave of "creative and intuitive insight". It muhstuh been the LORD; He who spoke the world into existence also whispered "Ebonics" in the ear of Dr. Williams, and it became a living, viable force. It had to be a moment of truth because all that is evil and all that is controversial and all that is negative has attempted to come against the realness of the concept Ebonics. His conceptualization was clear, and the defining of the term was clear – Clearly, then, there is no excuse for the African American child to still be left behind. As any good father does, Dr. Williams has stood by the term, Ebonics, as it has been criticized, damned, and hung, seemingly, on a cross of shame and degradation. That term, Ebonics, was made out of all that is Pure and Lasting, and it still stands today as the name for the 'true language of Black folks'. Ebonics has stood where the fals terms have had to attempt to change to fit the times: From Negro English to Black English to Black English Vernacular to African American English to African American Vernacular English . . ., the name Ebonics ain't gone nowhere, and it ain't going nowhere. From the fields of Arkansas to the halls of Washington University-St. Louis, Dr. Williams has taken his love for the Black children of this country before people of all walks of life. How can such an epiphany be dismissed as one man looking for vain glory? How can a lifetime spent in dedication to the cause of bettering the playing field for young Black children educationally and economically be viewed as one seeking self-acclaim? Thank you, Dr. Williams, for being a vessel.

SPECIAL TRIBUTE TO DR. ERNIE A. SMITH

Dr. Ernie A. Smith has got to be the one who created the word "mentor", for he has walked and talked and breathed the meaning of "mentor" for my professional growth as an Africologically-minded, Speech/Language Pathologist and researcher for the past twenty-four years. I admire his endurance as he walked me through many facets of Afrocentricity about which I was unlearned (and still am learning). The man is so much like another One Who was alone in His desire for all men to be free; Dr. Smith walks along a narrow trail with a few other soldiers, because, as many believe about that Other One Who came to bring a message of salvation to those lost in a world of sin, Dr. Smith is bringing a message of salvation for those lost in a world of illiteracy. Such messengers are often misunderstood and cast out, which makes them lead lonely lives. No, I do not claim that he *is* the Other One, but he is *as* the Other One, teaching as that One did, as one "having authority" to call out the uncleanness of hypocrites, and to call others dogs, Satan, perverse men, serpents, and vipers, when the needs for such shaking truths manifest themselves. As was with the Other One who was sent to teach, few wish to hear and adhere to Smith's teachings and wisdom. . . I know, however, that, if he was able to "save" me, the chief among all unlearned people concerning the language of slave descendants of African origin, his message may, also, spark something within others that will want them to cease being of *this* old mindset concerning Ebonics: That it is a language of poor, underprivileged, ignorant people who use a sloven, deviant, defective, broken form of English. He took an unformed and uninformed mind, and, praise God! After twenty-four years of intermittent though tedious training, I have been blessed to develop this first Work as a testament or tangible proof of Smith's excellent, scholarly teachings. Dr. Smith continues on and on and on and on with his 'sweat like blood' that runs down during his oratorical messages on the origin and historical development of Ebonics. Lastly, he has unwavering, permissible passion and, often times, righteous indignation, as he allows God to 'be his strength' in the saving of our children, and the educating of all who are willing to learn more about the language of the descendants of enslaved Africans in America—from the African side. Dr. "E.", you're alright with me.

TRIBUTE TO DR. MOLEFI KETE ASANTE

I hope to, one day, meet Dr. Asante face to face. I already know that he will be as he appears to be over the phone lines: Friendly, wise, caring, sharing, intellectually astounding, joyful, ambitious, and generous. Only such a man would put down his important work to take a few minutes to talk to me. That shows that he considers a person to be of worth, even if there are not a lot of alphabets behind her name. I grant it a privilege to have been accepted by Dr. Asante, and to have him grace this *Volume I* with the preface, for I *am* in awe of the alphabets behind his name, and the titles of his works that line the many walls of thousands of libraries in many lands. The thought of the prolificity of his pen makes my head want to spin; I cannot imagine one man having all of that word and knowledge power in his brain; Dr. Asante, the author!, Dr. Asante, the historian!, Dr. Asante, the journalist!, and Dr. Asante, the scholar!!, is living proof that the brain has the power to keep holding and holding and holding information – He is a special part of God, by God and for God, and I, therefore, thank God that Dr. Asante's example of learning and teaching was allowed on this sphere of existence.

TRIBUTE TO SOCIOLOGIST, DR. ADRIAN DOVE

I would be remiss if I did not take a few lines in this Work to thank Sociologist, Dr. Adrian Dove for *The Dove Counter Balance General Intelligence Test* (1968), which was nicknamed the *Soul Folk's Chitlin Test* (1968) by *Ebony Magazine, Jet Magazine,* and *The New York Times.* Reportedly, Dr. Dove's purpose 'was not an attempt to assess intelligence'. 'Neither was it to bring him fame or fortune'. In an interview Dr. Dove shared with me that he had become aware, and was concerned, that many Blacks were being denied public employment based on their scores on civil service examinations. Dr. Dove stated that he developed *The Dove Counter Balance General Intelligence Test* to give City, County, State and Federal personnel officers an idea of what it felt like to be assessed on test criteria that was culturally and linguistically foreign to them'. Dr. Dove's purpose was fulfilled: The cultural and linguistic bias was eased in that particular situation. I beseech all of the criticizers of this ingenious act to take the test, which was created for a specific purpose during that era. Now, today, our hats are off to Dr. Dove for letting the Lord use him to help his people. We thank him for drawing the blueprint for later tests that followed that, actually, purport to measure intellect in culturally sensitive ways. Again, Dr. Dove, I cannot thank you enough.

APPENDIX III

THE NAMING OF THIS BOOK

The naming of this Work was almost as tedious as the writing of this Work.

TENTATIVE BOOK TITLES

An Introduction to African American Language (Ebonics)

The Book of Ebonics: An Introduction

The Name of Ebonics

The New Lexicon of Ebonics (African American Language)

Taylor's Dictionary

The Word of Ebonics

A "Tanch" of Ebonics: As Viewed from a Southern Perspective

Ebonics: A Shelter from the Storm

Ebonics: As a Child Hears, So Speaks He

Ebonics: The Creative Invention of African Slaves, Their Children, . . .

Ebonics: The World Didn't Give It, The World Can't Take It Away

Ebonics vs. Black English

Saving Grace: How to Know if Your Mother Tongue Is Ebonics

From Generation to Generation: The Passing of Ebonics

Don't You Fool Yourself: Ebonics Might Be Your Mother Tongue

Appendix III: The Naming of this Book

Ebonics: The Language of Adam and Eve

Ebonics: The Fusion of African Grammar and English Words

Black Sounds: From the Phoneme to the Sentence

Introducing Ebonics: Black Sounds of Black People by Way of Africa

The Relexification of West and Niger Congo African Languages: Ebonics

And They Say Ebonics Is not a Language: The Buck-Naked Truth

Ebonics: The Full Legitimation of the African American Language System

Black Sounds Are not Black Sounds by Just Any Old, Other Name

Ebonics: Finally It's Out of the Closet. (Why Do You Wish to Stay There?)

Ebonics: The Retention of West and Niger-Congo African Languages in U.S. Slave Descendants

What God Has Joined Together, No Man Can Put Asunder: African Grammar and English Words

Ebonics: Were African Slaves and Their Descendants that Smart?

The Uncovering: Facts about Ebonics You Probably Don't Know

Ebonics, the Separation Line: People of African Ancestry from the Ape

Let Ebonics Ring!

Ebonics: An Imprint of West and Niger-Congo African Languages

The Roots of Ebonics

APPENDIX IV

RESOLUTION NO. 9697-0063 (OAKLAND UNIFIED SCHOOL DISTRICT

Full Text of the Original Resolution Adopting the Report and Recommendations of the African-American Task Force, passed on December 18, 1996

WHEREAS, numerous validated scholarly studies demonstrate that African American students as a part of their culture and history an African people possess and utilize a language described in various scholarly approaches as "Ebonics" (literally "Black sounds") or "Pan-African Communication Behaviors" of "African Language Systems"; and

WHEREAS, these studies have also demonstrated that African Language Systems are genetically based and not a dialect of English; and

WHEREAS; these studies demonstrate that such West and Niger-Congo African languages have been officially recognized and addressed in the mainstream public educational community as worth of study, understanding or application of its principles, laws and structures for the benefit of African-American students both in terms of positive appreciation of the language and these students' acquisition and mastery of English language skills; and

WHEREAS, such recognition by scholars has given rise over the past fifteen years to legislation passed by the State of California recognizing the unique language stature of descendants of slaves, with such legislation being prejudicially and unconstitutionally vetoed repeatedly by various California state governors; and

WHEREAS, judicial cases in states other than California have recognized the unique language stature of African-American pupils, and such recognition by courts has resulted in court-mandated educational programs which have substantially benefited African-American children in the interest of vindicating their equal protection of the law rights under the Fourteenth Amendment to the United States Constitution; and

WHEREAS, the Federal Bilingual Education Act (20 U.S.C. 1402 et seg.) mandates that local educational agencies "build their capacities to establish, implement and sustain programs of instruction for children and youth of limited English proficiency"; and

WHEREAS, the interests of the Oakland Unified School District in providing equal opportunities for all of its students dictate limited English proficient educational programs recognizing the English language acquisition and improvement skills of African-American students are as

fundamental as is application of bilingual educational principles for others whose primary languages are other than English; and

WHEREAS, the standardized tests and grade scores of African-American students in reading and language arts skills measuring their application of English skills are substantially below state and national norms and that such deficiencies will be remedied by application of a program featuring African Language Systems principles in instructing African-American children both in their primary language and in English; and

WHEREAS, standardized tests and grade scores will be remedied by application of a program with teachers and aides who are certified in the methodology of featuring African Language Systems principles in instructing African-American children both in their primary language and in English. The certified teachers of these students will be provided incentives including, but not limited to salary differentials,

NOW, THEREFORE, BE IT RESOLVED that the Board of Education officially recognizes the existence, and the cultural and historic bases of West and Niger-Congo African Language Systems, and each language as the predominantly primary language of African-American students; and

BE IT FURTHER RESOLVED that the Board of Education hereby adopts the report, recommendations and attached Pokily Statement of the District's African-American Task Force on language stature of African-American speech; and

BE IT FURTHER RESOLVED that the Superintendent in conjunction with her staff shall immediately devise and implement the best possible academic program for imparting instruction of African-American students in their primary language for the combined proposes of maintaining the legitimacy and richness of such language whether it is known as "Ebonics," "African Language Systems," "Pan-African Communication Behaviors" or other description, and to facilitate their acquisition and mastery of English language skills; and

BE IT FURTHER RESOLVED that the Board of Education hereby commits to earmark District general and special funding as is reasonably necessary and appropriate to enable the Superintendent and her staff to accomplish the foregoing; and

BE IT FURTHER RESOLVED that the Superintendent and her staff shall utilize the input of the entire Oakland educational community as well as state and federal scholarly and educational input in devising such a program; and

BE IT FURTHER RESOLVED, that periodic reports on the progress of the creation and implementation of such an educational program shall be made to the Board of Education at least once per month commencing at the Board meeting of December 18, 1996 (Perry & Delpit, 1998, p.143-145)

APPENDIX V

<u>REVISED EBONICS RESOLUTION NO. 9697-0063</u>
<u>OAKLAND UNIFIED SCHOOL DISTRICT</u>

Oakland Unified School District

Revisions are in Bold

WHEREAS, the numerous validated scholarly studies demonstrate that African-American students as a part of their culture and history **as** African people possess and utilize a language described in various scholarly approaches as "Ebonics" (literally "Black sounds") or "Pan-African Communication Behaviors" or "African Language Systems"; and

WHEREAS, these studies have also demonstrated that African Language Systems **have origins in West and Niger-Congo languages** and **are** not **merely dialects** of English; and

WHEREAS, these studies demonstrate that such West and Niger-Congo African languages have been recognized and addressed in the educational community as worthy of study, understanding **and** application of their principles, laws and structures for the benefit of African-American students both in terms of positive appreciation of the language and these students' acquisition and mastery of English language skills; and

WHEREAS, such recognition by scholars has given rise over the past fifteen years to legislation passed by the State of California recognizing the unique language stature of descendants of slaves, with such legislation being vetoed repeatedly by various California state governors; and

WHEREAS, judicial cases in states other than California have recognized the unique language stature of African American pupils, and such recognition by courts has resulted in court-mandated educational

155

programs which have substantially benefited African-American children in the interest of vindicating their equal protection of the law rights under the Fourteenth Amendment to the United States Constitution; and

WHEREAS, the Federal Bilingual Education Act (20 U.S.C. 1402 et seq.) mandates that local educational agencies "build their capacities to establish, implement and sustain programs of instruction for children and youth of limited English proficiency; and

WHEREAS, the interest of the Oakland Unified School District in providing equal opportunities for all of its students dictate limited English proficient educational programs recognizing the English language acquisition and improvement skills of African-American students are as fundamental as is application of bilingual **or second language learner** principles for others whose primary languages are other than English. **Primary languages are the language patterns children bring to school**; and

WHEREAS, the standardized tests and grade scores of African-American students in reading and language arts skills measuring their application of English skills are substantially below state and national norms and that such deficiencies shall be remedied by application or a program featuring African Language Systems principles **to move students from the language patterns they bring to school to English proficiency**; and

WHEREAS, standardized tests and grade scores will be remedied by application of a program that teachers and **instructional assistants**, who are certified in the methodology of African Language Systems principles **used to transition students from the language patterns they bring to school to English**. The certified teachers of these students will be provided incentives including, but not limited to salary differentials;

NOW, THEREFORE, BE IT RESOLVED that the Board of Education officially recognizes the existence, and the cultural and historic bases of West and Niger-Congo African Language Systems, and **these are the language patterns that** many African-American students **bring to school**; and

BE IT FURTHER RESOLVED that the Board of Education hereby adopts the report, recommendations and attached Policy Statement of the District's African-American Task Force on **the** language stature of African-American speech; and

BE IT FURTHER RESOLVED that the Superintendent in conjunction with her staff shall immediately devise and implement the best possible academic program for the combined purposes of facilitating **the acquisition and mastery of English language skills, while the respecting and embracing** the legitimacy and richness of the language **patterns** whether **they are** known as "Ebonics", "African Language Systems", "Pan-African Communication Behaviors", or other description; and

BE IT FURTHER RESOLVED that the Board of Education hereby commits to earmark District general and special funding as is reasonably necessary and appropriate to enable the Superintendent and her staff to accomplish the foregoing; and

BE IT FURTHER RESOLVED that the Superintendent and her staff shall utilize the input of the entire Oakland educational community as well as state and federal scholarly and educational input in devising such a program; and

BE IT FURTHER RESOLVED that periodic reports on the progress of the creation and implementation of such an educational program shall be made to the Board of Education at least once per month commencing at the Board meeting of December 18, 1996.

APPENDIX VI

LINGUISTIC SOCIETY OF AMERICA RESOLUTION ON THE OAKLAND EBONICS ISSUE (Adopted, unanimously, on January 3, 1997 in Chicago, Illinois)

Whereas there has been a great deal of discussion in the media and among the American public about the 18 December 1996 decision of the Oakland School Board to recognize the language variety spoken by many African American students and to take it into account in teaching Standard English, the Linguistic Society of America, as a society of scholars engaged in the scientific study of language, hereby resolves to make it known that:

> The variety known as "Ebonics," "African American Vernacular English" (AAVE), and "Vernacular Black English" and by other names is systematic and rule-governed like all natural speech varieties. In fact, all human linguistic systems—spoken, signed, and written—are fundamentally regular. The systematic and expressive nature of the grammar and pronunciation patterns of the African American vernacular has been established by numerous scientific studies over the past thirty years. Characterizations of Ebonics as "slang," "mutant," "lazy," "defective," "ungrammatical," or "broken English" are incorrect and demeaning.

> The distinction between "languages" and "dialects" is usually made more on social and political grounds than on purely linguistic ones. For example, different varieties of Chinese are popularly regarded as "dialects," though their speakers cannot understand each other, but speakers of Swedish and Norwegian, which are regarded as separate "languages," generally understand each other. What is important from a linguistic and educational

Appendix VI: Linguistic Society of American Resolution in the
Oakland Ebonics Issue

point of view is not whether AAVE is called a "language" or a "dialect" but rather that its systematicity be recognized.

As affirmed in the LSA Statement of Language Rights (June 1996), there are individual and group benefits to maintaining vernacular speech varieties and there are scientific and human advantages to linguistic diversity. For those living in the United States there are also benefits in acquiring Standard English and resources should be made available to all who aspire to mastery of Standard English. The Oakland School Board's commitment to helping students master Standard English is commendable.

There is evidence from Sweden, the US, and other countries that speakers of other varieties can be aided in their learning of the standard variety by pedagogical approaches which recognize the legitimacy of the other varieties of a language. From this perspective, the Oakland School Board's decision to recognize the vernacular of African American students in teaching them Standard English is linguistically and pedagogically sound.

APPENDIX VII

OVERVIEW OF VOLUME II

I challenge each person to consider the information shared in this Book, *Introduction to Ebonics, the Relexification of African Grammar with English and other Indo-European Words, Volume I.* If there was once any question about why Black students are not faring as well in the public school system as other students, or about why Black people have never seemed to "learn" English as other races of people have, then those questions should not continue to fester and destroy hopes of a change for Black students. For, now, everyone who has read *Volume I* has acquired the theoretical base and answer for what Ebonics is and what it is not. The publication of *Volume II* will solidify the foundation that has been laid, making this Work complete. The full gamut of the true language of Black folks, Ebonics, will be painted so vividly that everybody will want to sign up for a chance to help actuate a change in this country's public school system's teaching of Black children. Just know that, practically, "The best is yet to come;" or, in my mother tongue I will say, "You ain't seen nuh'ihn yet." The following is a preview of the chapters that will be in *Volume II.*

Chapter 6: Euro-American English Words, African American Meanings

Chapter 7: Semantically from the Black Mind

Chapter 8: Unique Phraseology

Chapter 9: Morpho-Syntactical Variations

Chapter 10: Idiomatic Phrases

Chapter 11: Recapitulation

Chapter 12: Amplifications

Chapter 13: Distinctive Sayings

Chapter 14: Proverbial Examples

Chapter 15: The Church Experience

Chapter 16: Interjections

Chapter 17: Language of the Sporting Life

Chapter 18: Conclusion of the Whole Matter

ABOUT THE AUTHOR

Linda Redmond Taylor, a native speaker of Ebonics, was born and reared in Jackson, Mississippi. Taylor is a contractual Speech/Language Pathologist, with the bulk of her clientele being students in the Shelby County School District of Memphis, Tennessee. She, also, is an entrepreneur (Vegan Food Designer for the family business, Right Stuff Health Systems). She graduated from the University of Mississippi in 1978 (*cum laude*) (where she pledged Delta Sigma Theta Sorority, Inc., and was the first musician for the now renowned University of Mississippi Gospel Choir for four years), with a Bachelor of Arts degree in Communicative Disorders. In 1991, she achieved a Master of Arts degree in Speech/Language Pathology (*cum laude*) at the, then, Memphis State University's Speech and Hearing Center, as the first recipient of the Minority Fellowship Grant Program.

Taylor is a member of the American Speech/Language and Hearing Association, holding the coveted Certificate of Clinical Competence (CCC) in Speech/Language Pathology; the National Black Association for Speech/Language and Hearing; and the University of Mississippi Alumni Association; and she is a serving board member to the Support and Training for Exceptional Parents, (STEP) Inc. of Tennessee. Taylor was honored by the University of Mississippi in 2015 with the Jennette Jennings "Trailblazer" Award.

Taylor's ultimate vision is to provide elective services to those who do not present a disorder (but who desire more competency in SAE without "jeopardizing the integrity of {his} first language") through their family ministry, Right Stuff Health Ministries. She envisions developing an enhancement center that will be geared toward Blacks who seek advancement in school, and those who aspire to achieve their optimum communicative capabilities in their selected fields of employment.

Taylor is married to Bro. Franco Taylor, and they are the parents of nine children in a blended family.

RELEVANT BIBLIOGRAPHY

Adler, S. (1993). *Multicultural Communication Skills in the Classroom.* Needham Heights, Massachusetts: Allyn and Bacon.

Alleyne, M. (1971). Linguistic Continuity of Africa in the Carribean. In R. Henry (Ed.), *Topics in Afro-American Studies.* New York: Black Academy Press.

Andrews, M. & Owens, P. (1973). *Black Language.* Los Angeles: Seymour-Smith.

Asante, M. (1990). African Elements in African-American English. In J. Holloway (Ed.), *Africanisms in American Culture.* Bloomington and Indianapolis: Indiana University Press.

_____. (1992). *Afrocentricity.* Trenton: Africa World Press, Inc.

American Speech-Language-Hearing Association. (1983). Social Dialects: A Position Paper. *ASHA, 25,* 23-24.

American Speech-Language-Hearing Association. (1985). Clinical Management of Communicatively Handicapped Minority Language Populations [Position Statement]. Available from www.asha.org/policy.

Baugh, J. (1983). *Black Street Speech: It's History, Structure, and Survival.* Austin: University of Texas Press.

Beale, P. (Ed.) (1989). *A Concise Dictionary of Slang and Unconventional English.* New York: Macmillan.

Beck, R. (Iceburg Slim) (1969). *Pimp: The Story of My Life.* Los Angeles: Holloway House Publishing Co.

Blackshire-Belay, C. (1996). "The Location of Ebonics Within the Framework of the Africological Paradigm." *Journal of Black studies, 27,* 5-23.

Boulware, M. (1969). *The Oratory of Negro Leaders: 1900 - 1968.* Connecticut: Negro Universities Press.

Brown, Les. (1997). *It's Not Over Until You Win!* New York: Simon & Schuster.

Bryson, B. (1990). *The Mother Tongue.* New York: William Morrow & Company.

Chomsky, N. (1972). *Language and Mind.* Harcourt Brace Jovanovich.

Cole, L. (1983). Implications of the Position on Social Dialects. *ASHA, 25,* 25-27.

Crawford, C. (2001). *Ebonics and Language Education.* Brooklyn: Sankofa World Publishers.

De Good Nyews Bout Jedus Christ wa Luke Write. (1995). New York: American Bible Society.

DeThorne, L.S. & Watkins, R.V. (2001). Listeners' Perceptions of Language Use in Children. *Language, Speech, and Hearing Services in Schools, 32,142-148.*

Dillard, J. L. (1972). *Black English: Its History and Usage in the United States.* New York: Vintage Books.

Douglass, F. (1962). *The Life and Times of Frederick Douglass.* Macmillan: New York.

Folb, E. (1980). *Running Down Some Lines.* Cambridge: Harvard University Press.

Fromkin, V. & Rodman, R. (1978). *An Introduction to Language.* New York: Holt, Rinehart, & Winston.

Greenburg, J. (1966). *Essays in Linguistics.* Chicago: University of Chicago Press.

Goldberg, B. (1997). Tailoring to Fit: Altering Our Approach to Multicultural populations. *ASHA, 39,* 23-28.

Hall, R., Jr. (1960). *Linguistics and Your Language.* Garden City, N.Y: Anchor Books.

Haskins, J. (1992). *I Have a Dream. The Life and Words of Martin Luther King, Jr.* Brookfield, CT: Millbrook Press.

Haskins, J. & Butts, H. (1973). *The Psychology of Black Language.* New York: Barnes & Noble.

Herskovitz, M. (1958). *Myth of the Negro Past.* (as originally published in 1941) Boston: Beacon Press.

Holloway, J. & Vass, W. (1993). *The African heritage of American English.* Bloomington & Indianapolis: Indiana University Press.

Jahn, J. (1961). *Muntu: The African Culture.* New York:

Joiner, C.W. (1979). E.D. Mich. July 12. *Martin Luther King Junior Elementary School Children v. Ann Arbor School District Board.* (Civil Action No. 7-71861).

Kenyon, J. S & Knott, T.A. (1953). *A Pronouncing Dictionary of American English.* Springfield: Merriam-Webster.

Key, M., Kollman, L., & Smith, E. (1971). "Features in Child Black English." In W. Mackey & T. Anderson (Eds.), *Bilingualism in Early Childhood.* Boston, Massachusetts: Newbury House.

Kifano, S. & Smith, E. (2000). Ebonics and Education in the Context of Culture: Meeting the Language and Cultural Needs of English Learning African American Students. In J. Ramirez, T.Wiley, G. Klerk, & E. Lee (Eds.), *Ebonics in the Urban Education Debate*. California: California State University.

Krapp, G. (1924). *The English of the Negro*. New York: American Mercury.

Major, C. (1971). *Dictionary of Afro-American Slang*. New York: International.

Mbiti, J. (1966). *African Oral Literature. Colloquium on Negro Art*. Senegal: The Society of African Culture.

McArthur, T. (Ed.) (1992). *The Oxford Companion to the English Language*. New York: Oxford University Press.

Merriam-Webster's Collegiate Dictionary, Eleventh Edition. (2009). Springfield: Merriam-Webster, Incorporated.

Merriam-Webster's Desk Dictionary. (1995). Springfield: Merriam-Webster, Incorporated.

Mintz, S. (2009-2015). "Facts about the Slave Trade and Slavery. The Gilder Lehrman Institute of American History. New York.

Mitchell, H. (1970). *Black Preaching*. New York: J.B. Lippincott.

Nehusi, K. (2001). From Medew Netjer to Ebonics. In C. Crawford (Ed.), *Ebonics and Language Education*. New York: Sankofa World Publishers.

Nunberg, G. (1997). Topic . . . Comment; Double Standards. *Natural Language & Linguistic Theory*, 15, 667-675.

O'Grady, W., Doborovolsky, M., & Arnoff, M. (1993). *Contemporary Linguistics: An Introduction.* New York: St. Martin's Press.

Okafor, V. (1997). "Toward an Africological Pedagogical Approach to African Civilization." *Journal of Black studies, 27, 299-317.*

Perry, T. & Delpit, L. (1998). *The Real Ebonics Debate.* Boston: Beacon Press Books.

Rickford, J. (2000). Using the vernacular to teach the Standard. In J. Ramirez, T. Wiley, G. de Klerk, and E. Lee (Eds.), *Ebonics in the Urban Education Debate.* Long Beach: California State University Center for Language Minority Education and Research.

Roberts, H. (1971). *The Third Ear: A Black Glossary.* The Better-Speech Institute of America.

Romaine, Suzanne. (2000). *Language in Society. Second Edition.* Oxford: Oxford University Press.

Sabree-Shakir, N. (2001). African Ancestry Students in America: Culturally-Relevant and Linguistially-Appropriate Professional Development, Curiculums and Instructional Strategies. In C. Crawford (Ed., *Ebonics and Language Education.* New York: Sankofa World Publishers.

Searle, C. (1972). *The Forsaken Lover.* London: Routledge & Kegan Paul.

Shabaka, S. & Smith, E.A. (2003). *Nigger: A Divine Origin.* Los Angeles: Milligan Books, Inc.

Simpkins, G. (2002). *The Throwaway Kids.* Brookline: Brooklin Books.

Smith, A. L. (Asante, M.) (1972). *Language, Communication, and Rhetoric in Black America.*

New York: Harper & Row.

Smith, E.A. *The Birth and Authentic Meaning of the Term Ebonics.* Unpublished article.

_____ (1974). *The Evolution and Continuing Presence of the African Oral Tradition in Black America.* Unpublished doctoral dissertation, University of California (Irvine).

_____ (1994). *The Historical Development of African American Language: The Africanist-Ethnolinguist theory. (Monograph).* Los Angeles: Watts College Press.

_____(1994). *The Historical Development of African American Language: The Pidgin Creole Hypothesis. (Monograph).* Los Angeles: Watts College Press.

_____(1994). *The Historical Development of African American Language: The Transformationalist Theory. (Monograph).* Los Angeles: Watts College Press.

_____ (1998). What is Black English? What is Ebonics? In T. Perry and L. Delpit (Eds.), *The Real Ebonics Debate: Power, Language, and the Education of African-American Children.* Boston: Beacon Press.

_____ (2001).Ebonics and Bilingual Education of the Afrian American Child. In C. Crawford (Ed.), *Ebonics and Language Education.* New York: Sankora World Publishers.

Smitherman, G. (1994). *BlackTalk: Words and Phrases From the Hood to the Amen Corner.* Boston: Houghton Mifflin.

_____ (2000). Black Language and the Education of Black Children: One Mo Once. In J. Ramirez, T. Wiley, G. de Klerk, and E. Lee (Eds.), *Ebonics in the Urban Education Debate*. Long Beach, California State University, Center for Language Minority Education and Research.

_____ (2001). Commentary on Ebonics: From a Ghetto Lady Turned Critical Linguist". In C. Crawford (Ed.), *Ebonics and Language Education*: New York: Sankofa World Publishers.

Tatum, A.W. (2005). *Teaching Reading to Black Adolescent Males*. Portland: Stenhouse Publishers.

The New Lexicon: Webster's Dictionary of the English Language (Vol. 2). (1992). New York: Lexicon Publications.

The Thompson Chain-Reference Bible (5th ed.). (1988). Indianapolis: B.B. Kirkbride Bible Co.

Turner, L. (1949). *Africanisms in the Gullah dialect*. Chicago: University of Chicago Press.

Twiggs, R. (1973). *Pan African Language in the Western Hemisphere*. Quincy, MA: Christopher Publishing.

Vass, W. K. (1979). *The Bantu Speaking Heritage of the United States*. Los Angeles: University of California.

Welmers, W.E. (1973). *African Language Structures*. Berkeley: University of California Press.

White, E.G. (1995). *Steps to Christ (African American Edition)*. Hagerstown, MD: Foy Institute Press.

White, E.G. (1985). *The Great Controversy Between Christ and Satan*. Altamont, TN: Pilgrim's Books.

Wiggins, M. (2014). *History of the National Black Association for Speech-Language and Hearing (NBASLH): The First Twenty Years, 1978 – 1998.* Norfolk: Poetica Publishing.

Wiley, T. (2000). Ebonics: Background to the Current Policy Debate. In J. Ramirez, T. Wiley, G. de Klerk, and E. Lee (Eds.), *Ebonics in the Urban Education Debate.* Long Beach: California State University, Center for Language Minority Education and Research.

Williams, R.L. (1975). *Ebonics: The True Language of Black Folks.* St. Louis: Institute of Black Studies.

_____(2001). Ebonics: Myths and Realities. In C. Crawford (Ed.), *Ebonics and Language Education.* New York: Sankofa World Publishers.

Wolfram, W. (1991). *Dialects and American English.* New Jersey: Prentice Hall.

Woodson, C.G. (1933). *The Mis-education of the Negro.* Washington, D.C: The Associated Publishers.

Wyatt, Toya A. (2000). Response to: Ebonics and Education in the Context of Culture. In J. Ramirez, T. Wiley, G. de Klerk, and E. Lee (Eds.), *Ebonics in the Urban Education Debate.* Long Beach, California State University, Center for Language Minority Education and Research.

www.ingramcontent.com/pod-product-compliance
Lightning Source LLC
Chambersburg PA
CBHW031259090426
42742CB00007B/518